The Vermont Monster Guide

THE

Vermont
Monster

GUIDE

Joseph A. Citro

Art by

Stephen R. Bissette

Eerie Lights Publishing
Eerielightspublishing.com

ISBN: 978-1-945950-19-3

EERIE LIGHTS
Eerie Lights Publishing
Eerielightspublishing.com

Cover design: Cayetano "Cat" Garza, Jr., and Stephen R.
Bissette based on a design concept by Joseph A. Citro
Cover illustrations: © 2009 Stephen R. Bissette, color by
Cayetano Garza, Jr.

Illustration page viii (top) reprinted courtesy of
the Crypto-Biological Collection of the First
Branch Memorial of the Main Street
Museum, Gulgo Vandersheltz Bargain,
conservator.

Contents

Introduction vii

Vermont Monster Hunting 101

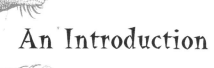

An Introduction

The geography of Vermont can be confusing.

At first everything might seem straightforward, snugly bordered as it is by New Hampshire, Massachusetts, New York, Lake Champlain, and Canada.

But there is another boundary that is rarely discussed.

If it were plotted on a map, it would appear as an undulating, serpentine line separating Vermont from The Land Beyond. You've probably seen that debatable land on old maps. It's an unexplored area designated with terrifying illustrations and captioned, "Here Monsters Dwell."

It is an area that won't be fenced-in or contained, an area that can't be perceived by ordinary human senses.

Usually.

Monsters seem to dwell on both sides of that line.

THE SEA SERPENT OF LAKE MEMPHREMAGOG AT COVE ISLAND. OWL'S HEAD AND MOUNT ELEPHANTIS IN THE DISTANCE.

On this side, glaciers receding some 10,000 years ago left behind evidence of mastodons, ancient whales, and other pre-historic animals unfamiliar in twenty-first-century Vermont. The proof is available and unambiguous: footprints, teeth, complete skeletons, fossils embedded in stone.

But on the other side, what dwells there? And what manner of beast travels freely back and forth between the two worlds?

For hundreds of years, Vermonters have been encountering odd critters on land, and in the air and water. Some have become old friends, like Champ, the monster of Lake Champlain. Some remain foreign and frightening, such as the awesome "Awful" up north around Richford, and the unbelievable monkey-men who tromp around down south.

Have you seen them?

Anyone who has hiked in the deep woods, explored a cave, or simply lounged beside a campfire swapping tales has felt close to that undiscovered country. Its proximity is disclosed not by signposts, spotlights, or radar, but by the simple experience of uneasiness or fear—sensations we have always associated with monsters.

In this book we will go on a monster hunt.

We will attempt to identify and inventory many of the creatures who dwell on both sides of the line—Vermont here and Vermont there. Some may be real (whatever that means). Some may be the product of imagination reinforced by repetition. And some may exist close by, near enough to breathe down our necks.

Better to meet them here than at night. On a lonely road. Or deep within some pitch-black forest.

Note

Any name with an asterisk (*) beside it is a pseudonym for a witness or reporter who chose not to be named.

WHAT LURKED IN THE DUCK POND IN DUXBURY, VERMONT?

LIKE MANY SMALL TOWNS AND VILLAGES WITH STANDING PONDS OR WATER-FILLED QUARRIES, LOCALS CLAIMED THERE WAS SOMETHING -- RUMORED TO BE AN OLD AND OUTSIZED SNAPPING TURTLE-- WAITING FOR UNWARY OR RECKLESS SWIMMERS...

From the beginnings of the ski industry, apocryphal "lodge tales" of unlikely and impossible cold-blooded creatures have been told.

Snow snakes and mogul monsters are still blamed for nasty falls and accidents on the slopes...

The Vermont Monster Guide

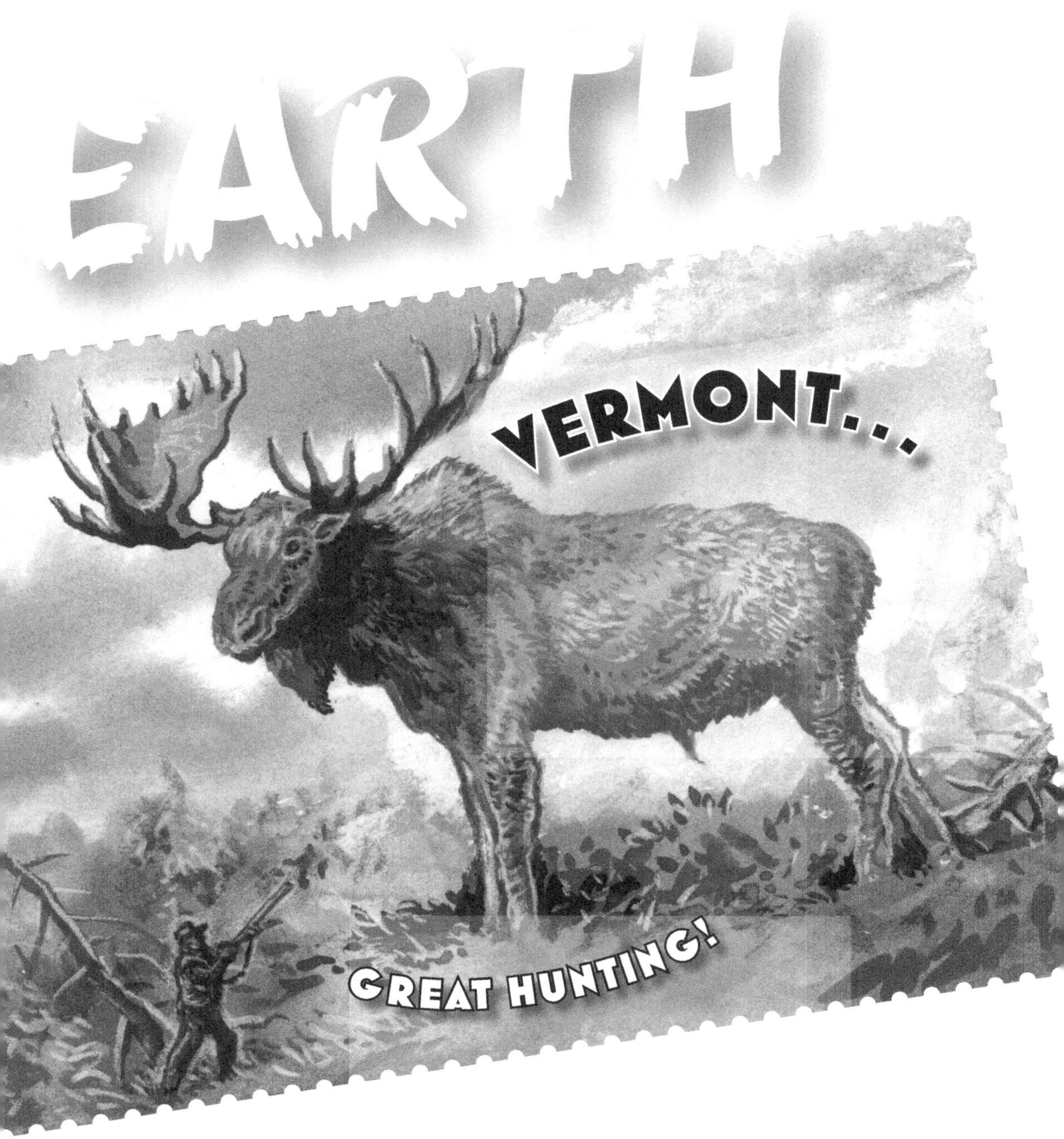
EARTH
VERMONT...
GREAT HUNTING!

PIGMAN

Northfield's Porcine Peculiarity

LOCATION: Northfield
DATE: 1971 to present

In 1971, citizens of Northfield knew something was wrong. A boy had vanished from a remote hill farm; he just blinked out of existence. Soon dogs, cats, and other animals were disappearing, too. A man on Turkey Hill heard something banging his trash cans around. What he saw paralyzed him with fear.

Days later, four terrified teenagers staggered into a high school dance—they said they had seen a monster!

Each had had a good look at it. Their descriptions matched the Turkey Hill witness's: The creature was big, tall as a man, stark naked, and covered head to foot with long, light-colored hair. Whatever it was raced away on two feet.

But the scariest thing was its face. There was nothing human about it. Contrary to all experience and logic, it had the hideous features of a pig.

More curious encounters followed. Many occurred between an old pig farm near Union Brook and a dark, wet woodland known as "The Devil's Washbowl."

Upon exploration, crude bedding was discovered at both locations . . . along with piles of bones and the half-devoured carcasses of cats, dogs, and other small animals. It appeared that something had made its home first at a pig-barn, then relocated to the caves at "Devil's Washbowl."

People passing the Washbowl at night reported unidentifiable howls and screams; many saw a fleet white "something" dart past their headlights and into the woods. Once, the creature jumped onto a vehicle's hood, scaring the poor driver half to death. Again, its most memorable feature was the hideous pig-like face.

When a young couple went parking near the Washbowl, their evening of bliss turned to horror. As the boy got out to answer nature's call, something seized him, pummeled him, and hurled him against his car. The shaken youth added another detail to the monster's description: The creature's hands were not like those of a pig. Or a man. It had long nails like claws. Prints found in the moist soil suggested "cloven" or hoofed feet.

Now the creature's crimes had escalated from animal snatching to assault. Local police investigated, but found nothing.

In time, the "Pigman" appeared less frequently, then not at all. Quite possibly, he eventually died of starvation, suicide, or a hunter's bullet. Or perhaps he's still

3

there, now in middle age, skilled at concealment and far too cautious ever to show himself.

The mystery is not so much where he went, but where he came from in the first place. And why? How can we account for his bizarre behavior and grotesque appearance? What, we must ask, could cause such a monster to be?

Descriptions of the Pigman were always the same. It looked like a person but had that preposterous pig-like face. The porcine phantom stood a good five foot eight to five foot ten. He walked upright. His body was naked and completely covered with light, maybe white, hair. Pigman had long claws, possibly cloven feet. It could move very fast!

SEE ALSO: Batboy, Human-Faced Calf

MONSTER CATS

LOCATION: Various
DATE: Prehistory to present

It is not unusual to see cats in Vermont. They scratch in every yard, snooze on every porch, and torture small chipmunks and mice.

But *monster cats* are another story.

Large mystery felines have been spotted all over the state. They are called catamounts, mountain lions, cougars, giant panthers—and there's the other mysterious subset of long-legged cats, unheard of in this region. All have one thing in common: they're not supposed to be here.

But giant cats four to seven feet long have been seen regularly since long before the alleged "last catamount" was shot by Alexander Crowell in Barnard back in 1881.

Today the question is, do such creatures still roam Vermont hills?

Authorities say no, yet people keep seeing them. I saw one myself back in 1991 while traveling with a companion north on Route 89. It was late afternoon; the road was clear with plenty of light. Near Bethel, we saw something crossing the road. As we got closer, it became clearer. There could be no doubt about what it was. The mega-cat stopped at the roadside, glanced casually at our oncoming car, then sprang into the bushes.

Catamounts are back. They lived here once, maybe now they only visit. Generally they're harmless; they just appear and vanish, leaving witnesses scratching their heads. But occasionally these monstrous entities leave their mark—and it's worse than scratched tree trunks, paw prints, or scat.

5

For example, over four days in late October 1991, something attacked livestock in an Orwell barn. Fourteen heifers and one cow were mutilated, their sinuses crushed, their faces sliced to ribbons. Obviously the culprit was something big.

Farmer Kenneth Pope and veterinarian Dr. Kent Anderson concluded a large cat was responsible, a cat bigger than a house cat, bobcat, or lynx.

The notion was reinforced because the mutilated animals were left alive. Cats have a habit of playing with prey. They will attack without killing.

SEE ALSO: Black Panthers, Long-Leggedy Cats

BLACK PANTHERS

LOCATION: Montpelier, various
DATE: 1946 and others

Although catamounts were business as usual in the old days, another feline phantom has never been native to Vermont. It's not here; it never has been here, yet seemingly unambiguous reports occasionally drift in. These are black panther sightings.

I spoke with Marian Peduzzi of Montpelier, who had an unforgettable confrontation back in 1946. Although many other sightings have been reported since then, Mrs. Peduzzi's was especially dramatic.

She was sixteen years old at the time. At about four o'clock one afternoon, she was heading home for supper, walking along Vine Street, a dirt road near U.S. 302.

Movement caught her eye. At first she thought she was seeing a black Labrador. "Then" she says, "I saw it scratching backwards with its hind legs at the ground. Strange behavior for a dog . . ."

Then she realized it wasn't a dog—in fact, it was nothing she had ever seen before. She detoured toward her friend Mrs. Tiffin's house, walking with tremendous caution. "The wind was blowing my way," she said. "My heart was pounding. If that cat could smell me and wanted a meal, then I'd be trapped."

She climbed the porch steps and called. "Mrs. Tiffin! Mrs. Tiffin!"

When Mrs. Tiffin opened the door, she saw it too.

The cat, glossy and sleek in the afternoon sun, was about four feet long, with a long tail that curved toward the ground. It stood up and loped directly toward the house as the women cringed. Then it veered to the right and cantered parallel to the road until it vanished.

For the rest of her life, Mrs. Peduzzi swore that she had seen "a Vermont black panther, a catamount, in all its glory."

SEE ALSO: Long-Leggedy Cats, Monster Cats

OLD SLIPPERYSKIN

LOCATION: Lemington, Morgan, Maidstone, Victory, Westmore and others
DATE: circa 1800

Old Slipperyskin is one of the earliest BHMs (Big Hairy Monsters) to be reported in Vermont. In the region now known as the Northeast Kingdom, early settlers had repeated run-ins with a fearsome oddity that kept them in constant fear. The monster seemed impervious to bullets and impossible to trap. It was dubbed "Old Slipperyskin" because it always slipped away when anyone tried to capture it.

So what was it? Some people said it resembled a huge bear, but unlike any known bear it always walked upright, on two legs, just like a person. Apparently it was gigantic, with legs the size of spruce logs and footprints as big as wagon wheels.

In her *History of Lemington, Vermont*, Marion M. Daley wrote that Old Slipperyskin "terrorized this part of the country for many years and committed wholesale destruction. He was a mean animal, and evidently had a grudge against humans. He destroyed their fences, ripped up their gardens, frightened their cows and sheep, tromped through the corn fields and caused no end of mayhem."

Then she described its unnatural cleverness. "For maliciousness and cunning," she wrote, "it was claimed he would never be compared, except to humans. He seemed to enjoy himself immensely, frightening people and livestock, kicking over manure piles and throwing stones into machinery left in fields."

Slipperyskin also seemed to target specific individuals for revenge, people who had in some way offended it. It might fill their sap buckets with rocks, knock over their woodpiles, use logs to spring their traps, even throw stones at—or otherwise terrify—their children.

It would then disappear by carefully backtracking in its own prints, leaving a trail that seemed to end abruptly, suggesting that it had just vanished.

The beast was most active in Morgan, Maidstone, Lemington, and Victory. Over time, reports became less frequent and eventually stopped. People presumed that the creature had died or gone back to wherever it had come from. But continuing news of similar alien animals from elsewhere around Vermont suggests that Old Slipperyskin's offspring may still be with us.

SEE ALSO: Bennington Monster, Bigfoot, Forest Wanderer, Goonyak, Windigo

A Vermont Monster Hunter

When he was campaigning for governor in 1815, Jonas Galusha heard the weird tales about Old Slipperyskin. A number of organized hunts had attempted to rid the North Country of the mysterious menace, but all had failed.

Governor Galusha vowed to kill it once and for all.

Known as an excellent hunter, he gathered a group of men and entered the Maidstone woods where the beast had last been seen.

Governor Galusha—so the story goes—had a plan that had never been tried before. He lathered himself up with an ointment said to contain the scent of female bear. Then, gun in hand, he set out to stalk the pesky critter. Shortly, Governor Galusha came whooping and bellowing back into camp screaming, "Outta my way boys, I'm bringin' him back alive!"

Old Slipperyskin was in hot pursuit!

The other hunters scattered. No one thought to shoot. And, as usual, the beast eluded capture.

GOONYAK

LOCATION: Morrisville, Wolcott, Craftsbury, and environs

DATE: 1978

Another BHM (Big Hairy Monster), Goonyak killed a farmer's bull and tried to carry it off. The whole story turned out to be bull, but we like the critter's name, so we've included it.

SEE ALSO: Bennington Monster, Bigfoot, Forest Wanderer, Fur-Bearing Trout, Human-Faced Calf, Old Slipperyskin, Windigo

KING MOOSE

LOCATION: the North Country   **DATE**: Ongoing

For years, in the northernmost counties of Vermont, hunters, loggers, and outdoorspersons have swapped stories about the "King Moose," a supernaturally large animal observed by very few people. This moose is almost twice the size of a conventional moose. Its weight is sometimes estimated as over 2,500 pounds. It has antlers spreading ten feet and is fifteen feet tall at the shoulders. This north woods monster has also been spotted in Maine and New Hampshire. It's described as dusky white, even pure white in color. A number of hunters claim to have shot it, but, unfazed by bullets, it walks away. Its coloration and apparent longevity may have led to its alternate name: The Ghost Moose.

SEE ALSO: Giant Red-Eyed Rabbits, His Snakeship, King Bullfrog, Old Ironsides

HIS SNAKESHIP

LOCATION: Richmond, Woodstock, Bethel, and others
DATE: Ongoing

During the nineteenth century, newspapers often ran accounts of giant snakes. Editors competed to see who could report the biggest snake, especially in areas like Vermont where such critters should be impossible. These stories were so frequent that their subjects took on nicknames such as "Boss Snake" and "His Snakeship."

In the nineteenth century, a Mr. T. Owsley reported one in the Taconic Mountains of southern Vermont. It was, he said, "as large as a common stove-pipe and about twelve feet long." The *Troy (NY) Post* claimed that it was, "The largest snake ever heard of in this part of the world. . ."

On Wednesday, July 22, 1878, the *New York Times* reported that William Fields of Richmond—"a truthful, sober man"—was visiting the farm of his neighbor Jonathan Fay when he was startled to see "two large snakes the color of boa-constrictors." He said, "They were full six feet long, and when they saw me they raised their heads and opened their mouths and darted out their tongues." He claims they were as thick as his arm. The newspaper adds, "Mr. Fields did not stop to interview them."

In that same neck of the woods, and at roughly the same time, Dr. Bromley was making his rounds when he saw what appeared to be a rail across the road. But it was moving!

The snake, Dr. Bromley estimated, was a good ten feet long.

Around 1940, Betty Paige of Woodstock was driving at night on a local dirt road when she saw a giant snake in her headlights. It extended completely across the road and into the underbrush. She stopped and watched it until it was out of the way. Then she sped home.

Another twentieth-century account is from Bethel, circa 1953. Eleven-year-old Lori Kearns* was walking along a partially grown-over wagon path near her home. She says, "I saw something up in front of me stretched along the pathway laying in some sunlight coming through a break in the big maple trees." At first she thought she was seeing some kind of colorful garden hose, but it was way too big for that. As she looked, it moved! She thought, *Glory Be, it's a huge snake!* But she quickly tried to talk herself out of that notion.

Lori had never seen anything like it. Multi-colored, with swirling, blending browns, reds, yellows, and blacks, it left her greatly puzzled as she tried to compute its size. The snake stretched across the path—a width of at least seven feet—with perhaps another foot on either side vanishing into the goldenrods. That would make it at least seven feet long! She says it was as big around as her lower leg, making its girth somewhere between five and seven inches. She says, "I have tried looking up photos of the snake I saw that afternoon, but never found one which looked exactly the same."

Such a weird serpent doesn't seem natural in Vermont. Can such "unnatural" things be slithering through the Green Mountains in the twenty-first century?

14

What to Do if Attacked

The following is adapted from what purports to be the U.S. Government Peace Corps Manual for volunteers working in the Amazon jungle. It details what to do if an anaconda attacks you. The anaconda is the largest snake in the world, growing to thirty-five feet and weighing 300 to 400 pounds.

Although no Vermont snake is known to attain that size, the techniques described might apply if a local Boss Snake unexpectedly manifests and decides to attack:

1 If you are attacked by a giant snake, do not run. The snake is faster than you are.
2 Lie flat on the ground. Put your arms tight against your sides, your legs tight against one another.
3 Tuck your chin in.
4 The snake will begin to nudge and climb over your body.
5 Do not panic.
6 After the snake has examined you, it will begin to swallow you from the feet end—always from the feet end. Permit the snake to swallow your feet and ankles. Repeat: Do not panic!
7 The snake will now begin to suck your legs into its body. You must lie perfectly still. This will take a long time.
8 When the snake has reached your knees, slowly and with as little movement as possible, reach down, take your knife, and very gently slide it into the side of the snake's mouth between the edge of its mouth and your leg, then suddenly rip upwards, severing the snake's head.
9 Be sure you have your knife.
10 Be sure your knife is sharp.

OLD IRONSIDES

LOCATION: Mount Ascutney
DATE: Year after year

Tom Kenyon of the West Windsor Historical Society recalls the story of Old Ironsides, the forest phantom of Mount Ascutney: "Many, many years ago, before hunting rifles had scopes, just open sights, in the town of West Windsor there was 'Old Ironsides,' which was a huge buck (some years he had twelve points, some years more). No one could bring down that buck even with multiple shots. Old Ironsides was a native buck, not one of them skinny white-tailed deer. He lived most of the time up on the side of Mount Ascutney. No one kept track of how many hunters had seen that 'bullet-proof deer' in a local field, had shot and shot at him, and all had missed bagging that big old buck. It was always interesting to note the hunter was always by himself, not one witness. Often the hunter would say he was sure he hit 'Old Ironsides' and when he tried to track him, that old smart buck always went over onto posted land [where no hunting was allowed]. Sadly, most of the hunters who shot and missed 'Old Ironsides' are getting old now and can no longer get out in the woods to hunt. On the bright side, however, many of those hunters can remember new fresh details each time they tell their 'Old Ironsides' story."

Mr. Kenyon concludes his account by saying, "I know other towns have had their versions of Ironsides, the difference of course is that we can look up at the side of Ascutney Mountain and know he is there, and we know he often looks down on us through the year. We wonder if during hunting season he is just over the hill or up near the peak of Ascutney looking down knowing he is safe."

SEE ALSO:
King Moose

The HOPPING HORROR

LOCATION: East Dorset, Manchester, and environs
DATE: 1999 to present?

A certain stretch of Route 7 near Manchester is known for nocturnal sightings of a naked, hopping, man-like critter that sometimes moves "like a gorilla." It is light in color and not described as "hairy." Witnesses say it seems to be more creature than human.

At about 12:45 a.m. on Friday, August 20, 1999, forty-four-year-old Terri Geer* was driving to her Danby home from her job inspecting fly rods at the Orvis manufacturing plant in Manchester. Terri is a multi-generational Vermonter with adult sons. In general, she is well acquainted with her neighbors, human and animal. But what she saw that Friday night she could only describe as "crazy."

She said, "I've never seen the like in my life!" Her Geo Metro had just passed the entrance to Emerald Lake State Park, headed north on Route 7. Terri always watched carefully for wildlife on this straight stretch of road. When she saw something crossing the road—east to west—she thought it was a deer. Until she saw it hop! As she got closer, the hopping stopped and a gorilla-like shambling began. "When it reached the other side of the road," Terri said, "it threw itself into the ditch" and vanished.

Terri says that whatever it was stood no more than six feet tall, was flesh colored or very light, making it appear hairless, and had extremely long arms. She attributes the "hopping motion" to the elongated arms, saying it moved, "the way a gorilla moves, with its extra-long arms helping to propel it along."

Later, Terri checked with some fellow workers, Roy and Betty N., who had taken the same route home. She was surprised to discover that they had also seen something weird, and were equally baffled. It was crossing the same stretch of road, east to west, suggesting that at least two of the Hopping Horrors may be roaming the woods of southern Vermont.

SEE ALSO: Bigfoot, Old Slipperyskin, Woodman

FOREST WANDERER

LOCATION: Any deep woods
DATE: Prehistoric to present

Of all the terrifying creatures known to the Native Americans, the most feared was the Forest Wanderer, a giant cannibal who didn't hesitate to feed upon anyone unlucky enough to cross his path. In fact, if he gets hungry, absolutely nothing will stop him from chowing down on the closest human prey. If an Indian hunter spotted the Forest Wanderer's footprints in the snow or soil, the whole village would evacuate immediately in terror.

Another name for—or perhaps close relative of—the Forest Wanderer is Windigo. The Wanderer or Windigo is so frightful that native peoples developed what is called the "Windigo psychosis." This mental disorder, identified among northern Algonquins, may be the root of the Forest Wanderer and Windigo stories. The victim of the psychosis experiences an escalating, uncontrollable craving for human flesh. The urge can get so strong that it must be acted upon. The grisly outcome can be vividly imagined. However, in their book *The Original Vermonters*, William A. Haviland and Marjory W. Power report, "To our knowledge, no instance of Windigo psychosis has ever been reported for Abenakis, eastern or western." Whew!

SEE ALSO: Bennington Monster, Bigfoot, Goonyak, Old Slipperyskin, Windigo

LOCATION: Anywhere

DATE: Ongoing

Something is lurking in the Vermont wilds that seems as much ghost as monster. Called Shadow People (or alternately, Shadow Beings, Shadow Men, and sometimes Elementals), these creatures may be in a category of their own. They have the general shape of a person, usually male, but appear as three-dimensional shadows with no recognizable features. Often they seem to have smoke or mist rising from them.

They like to watch people, but generally will flee if spotted. When they are seen, the percipient most likely will dismiss them as misperceptions.

Certain individuals experience recurring contact with Shadow People. Since she was a child, Sonya Shore* of Hartford has had frequent encounters with these dark, insubstantial beings. Generally, she sees them while hiking in the woods where, she says, they hang out "in trees and areas where water makes a dark pool, such as at the base of a tree in a stream." But sometimes they enter her house by traveling through the glass of her bedroom window. She perceives them as "shifting moving shadows that have a slightly 'pixilated' texture to them."

Sonya tells of an especially dramatic encounter as recently as the summer of 2008: "I was playing my flute at night, standing in the garage, looking outside into the night. As I played, I could see shapes moving from the road and woods up our driveway and lawn. . . . So I decided to stop playing and watch. They quickly cavorted back to the woods and I went inside. It appears they like music."

Although these music-loving silhouettes may be harmless, seeing one can be a terrifying experience.

SEE ALSO: Little People

SHADOW PEOPLE

BIGFOOT

24

LOCATION: Statewide
DATE: Prehistory to the present

Although this infamous BHM (Big Hairy Monster) generally is associated with the Pacific Northwest, Bigfoot is nonetheless the king of Vermont land monsters. First known to the Native Americans, then to the Europeans, this oversized hairy humanoid is still confronted today. Researchers speculate that it keeps to the sparsely populated Northeast Kingdom, but it has been seen as far south as Bennington and Pownal.

In 1609, Samuel de Champlain heard Native American stories of oversized, hairy men who hid in the dense woods. In 1759, Roger's Rangers encountered an incredible creature that fits Bigfoot's description. On October 18, 1879, a "wild man" sighting near Pownal made front-page news in the *New York Times*. And in 1977, Bigfoot's likeness was photographed on forest service property in Chittenden.

Since then, he, she, or it is still sighted with alarming regularity, even in developed parts of the state. For example, in April 1984, James Guyette saw a "huge hairy animal-man" walking on Interstate 91 within sight of the Hartland Dam. In September 2003, Ray Dufresne and three other witnesses saw a similar man-beast beside Route 7 between Bennington and Manchester.

More recently, in May 2006, two thirteen-year-old cousins were visiting their grandparents' cabin in Marshfield. Zooming on ATVs along a forgotten logging road, they halted before a fallen tree. As they were reversing direction, a creature— seven feet tall and hairy—rose, spotted them, and fled into the forest.

So what's out there? Who will see it next? The evidence to date—whether anecdotal or physical—just isn't enough. And Bigfoot, be it real, hoax, or misperceived shadows, remains a living mystery.

SEE ALSO: Bennington Monster, Forest Wanderer, Goonyak, Old Slipperyskin, Windigo

WEREWOLF

LOCATION: Groton Pond, northern Vermont, and elsewhere
DATE: Nineteenth century to present

This French-Canadian monster slipped across the border from Quebec using the name *loup-garou*. Although he's not one of Vermont's better-known creatures of the night, he still puts in an appearance now and then. In his article "Mountains Top Off New England" (*National Geographic Magazine*, May 1951), F. Barrows Colton tells how his father and uncle owned a hunting and fishing camp on Groton Pond. At that time, the pond was in the heart of Vermont's lonely mountain wilderness. On one trip to the cabin, they brought along Joe Leblanc, a French-Canadian logger, whom they had hired to chop firewood. Known as an excellent and energetic worker, Joe was chopping away as the men headed out to fish. When they returned a few hours later, Joe wasn't there. However, they found his coat, hat, and, strangest of all for a true woodsman, his ax.

Mr. Barrows writes, "He finally turned up at a near-by sawmill village with a wild look in his eyes. In the woods, he had seen the awful *loup-garou* and had got out of there fast."

Mr. Leblanc's terror is understandable to anyone who knows the French-Canadian legend. A *loup-garou*, they say, is a kind of werewolf. Basically, it's a man who has been transformed into a wolf (or possibly some other animal) as a punishment for serious wrongdoing. This flesh-hungry mangler has dark hair attached to a skin that's impervious to bullets, knives, even axes—unless the weapon has been blessed. Only a blessed weapon—like a shotgun filled with rosary beads—can kill the dreaded *loup-garou*.

A more recent encounter was reported in 2006. A woman named Tonya experienced what she believes was a werewolf confrontation in a populated part of northern Vermont. After working an extra shift at her factory job, she drove home about three o'clock in the morning. The moon was full and her headlights were working perfectly. She slowed down as she passed through a residential neighborhood with a posted speed limit of 30 miles per hour.

When she caught motion at the side of the road, she slowed down some more, not wanting to collide with some family pet. What she saw was like a house pet

26

from hell! An enormous, four-legged animal was loping along beside her car. Occasionally it would leer at her, face to face, as she looked back. It wasn't a dog, she knew that right away. But what was it?

Dagger-like teeth protruded from its oversized muzzle. Its eyes glowed red. And it easily kept pace with her car, although she sped up to well past the speed limit.

Then, Tonya says, things became more frightening. She saw a second creature alongside her, and a third in her rearview mirror. She was being surrounded! Instinct flared! They were trying to cut her off! She says, "I finally knew what any wild rabbit knows: the feeling of being hunted."

She screamed and hit the gas, speeding out of the neighborhood at nearly 70 miles per hour. A glance in the rearview mirror told her that she had the advantage; the animals were fading into the distance.

But to this day she is sure they were not dogs. Or wolves. Tonya is convinced that she was pursued by a pack of northern Vermont werewolves.

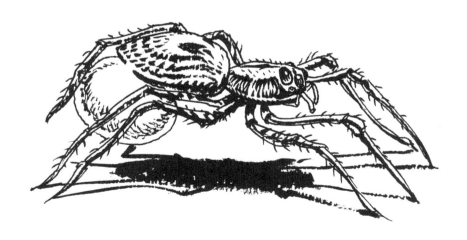

GIANT RED-EYED RABBITS

LOCATION: Lake Bomoseen, Rutland County   **DATE**: Ongoing

Stories about Giant Rabbits just don't go away!

Any night, some Rutland County resident might spot one hopping across a dirt road or bounding among the trees. They are distinctive not only because of their size but also for their red, glowing eyes. How they got here is a mystery, because all the Giant Rabbits in Vermont are supposed to be confined to an island in Lake Bomoseen. Tales of these over-large Leporidae may date back to Abenaki days, but the sightings persist. Contemporary vacationers often take boat rides around the island, shining their flashlights into the vegetation, hoping to spot a giant hopper. Perhaps that's why their stomping ground is called Rabbit Island.

How did they get there? The legend illustrates a Darwinian principle. The only access to the island is a thirty-foot jump, shore to island. So only big rabbits could make it. Once there, they couldn't get back, so they stayed put and did what rabbits do: multiplied. Over the years, they produced stronger, bigger progeny. Some are the size of Saint Bernards, some grow to be as big as Volkswagens.

No one has ever accused these giant rabbits of doing any harm, but most people agree they would not make good pets. And a confrontation with one could be pretty harey.

29

LITTLE PEOPLE

LOCATION: Various
DATE: Ongoing

These mini-monstrosities, the Little People, are "people" in name only. Some live underwater, like the Manogemassak, who are a bit evil, although that is offset by their shyness. It is better to avoid them, but if you encounter one, it will take off, being more afraid of you then you are of it. Those who have seen them say they have extremely thin faces, "like ax blades." They speak in low, squeaky voices that are quite chilling to the human ear. These Little People work at night, performing inexplicable tasks, such as crafting round stones identical to those found at Button Bay on Lake Champlain.

A modern explanation of these quasi-human critters suggests that they might be "interdimensional," or at least two-dimensional, because they can be seen if viewed from the front, but if they turn sideways, they vanish.

Native Abenaki Little People, the Mikumwesu, are very powerful. They are tasked with defending the world against monsters. Iroquois Little People (Djo-ge-oh) guard the entrances to caves that lead to inner earth, where monsters are penned up so they cannot hurt people. In this way, the Djo-ge-oh seem to help mankind. However, they also will defend their territory from trespassing humans. So to them maybe, *we* are the monsters.

In certain Native Americans traditions—as in the Celtic Fairy Faith—even talking about the Little People is frowned upon and considered dangerous.

So maybe we should stop here.

SEE ALSO: Shadow People

LOCATION: Northern Vermont

DATE: Ongoing

"WINDIGO: Man-eating wilderness god of North American Indian legend. Specific descriptions of this horrifying apparition vary slightly from tribe to tribe.

"Always described as huge, and sometimes as gigantic, the Windigo is thought to be a naked manlike creature horribly disfigured by its unending exposure to the elements.

"Compelled by preternatural forces, the Windigo runs maniacally through the limitless forests, stopping only to feed on tribesmen who have become lost.

"The legend of the Windigo has survived many generations and, surprising though it is, continues until this day. As recently as 1986, many people claim to have heard the Windigo rustling through the bush in the forests of northern Quebec and the Pacific Northwest. The fearsome creatures are said to utter terrifying hissing sounds, whistles, or loud, sinister howls that will strike fear in the hearts of anyone, even the most seasoned woodsmen.

"The Windigo is said to have a limited human vocabulary, usually restricted to the name of its next victim.

"It is commonly believed that the Windigo will, for reasons known only to itself, mark certain individuals for transformation. It will then summon the victim simply by calling his name. When called, the victim is compelled to obey. This 'naming' begins the process by which the Windigo magically transforms humans into its own likeness.

"Some legends hold that the transformation from man to Windigo can also originate through an act of flesh-eating. If, while in the woods, a human being consumes the flesh of another human, the change will begin.

"Many folklorists believe that Windigo legends arose from the American Indian's strong cultural aversion to cannibalism. In the severe northern winters the threat of being visited by, or changing into, a Windigo may have kept many individuals from turning to cannibalism, especially during times of famine."

⇛ from *An Omnibus of Evil Gods*, by L. Connelly Bronson (1990)

Alternately called Wendigo, Weendigo, Windago, Windiga, Witiko, Wihtikow, and numerous other variants.

SEE ALSO: Bennington Monster, Bigfoot, Forest Wanderer, Goonyak, Old Slipperyskin

WINDIGO

33

The PURPLE HAND

LOCATION: Plymouth
DATE: 1860 to present

Did something wet and heavy plop onto your shoulder? Is something cold and clammy crawling around in your sleeping bag? Better hope it's not the Purple Hand!

When we were kids at Boy Scout Camp in Plymouth (now Camp Plymouth State Park), tales of the Purple Hand kept us awake and trembling all night.

We knew one thing was true: that Vermont's gold rush took place in Plymouth during the latter half of the nineteenth century. The deserted mines are still there to prove it. So, we reasoned, tales of the Purple Hand must also be true.

It all began with a hard-working miner who struck it rich in his little, out-of-the-way claim somewhere in the rugged cliffs of Plymouth Five Corners. He worked alone, morning till night, and was able to stash a tidy sum.

But he was being watched. A less honest, less ambitious miner was spying on him, hoping to learn the location of the gold. Eventually, the villain confronted the miner, and tied him to a big tree in front of his cabin. He tried to force the miner to reveal the location of his mine. Finally the villain resorted to torture. When all else failed, he took an axe and severed of the miner's hand. Still tied to his tree, the miner bled to death without ever revealing the location of his gold. The villain dragged the body off and toppled it down a disused mine shaft. But when he returned to the cabin, the hand was no longer on the ground.

It had crawled off like a five-legged spider and hidden among some rocks. There, due to oxygen deprivation, it slowly turned a purplish color.

The villain took up residence in the dead miner's cabin. One night, he heard a tapping outside. He figured it must be raccoons, so he thought no more about it. That is, until something burst through the window.

It was the Purple Hand. It quickly affixed itself to the man's throat and throttled the life out of him.

When the body was discovered, everyone figured it was the work of the cabin's owner, who was missing.

But ever since then, the Purple Hand has remained animated, crawling through the forests and swamps around Plymouth, groping blindly for its next victim.

QUETZALCOATL

LOCATION: Johnson

DATE: 1971

Do demons manifest in backwoods Vermont? Can amateur occultists conjure ancient monsters to do their bidding?

In 1971, Johnson State College student David R.* found himself reluctantly drawn into unusual events surrounding a campus coven of witches. His initial involvement was peripheral. "I had no interest in what they were up to," David recalls, "but it began to impact those around me—and not in good ways."

Late one afternoon, David found himself very involved as he drove a classmate away from campus—and in a hurry. His panicked friend claimed to have been targeted by the coven; he was fleeing from a threat that he was either unable to comprehend, or was too frightened to describe.

Skeptical but concerned—and frankly worried that the terrified fellow might hurt himself—David rushed to get them far away from Johnson before night fell. They stuck to the back roads to avoid any possible chase or confrontation.

Then *something* stopped them in their tracks.

"It crossed the road right in front of us," David recalls, "and I slammed on the brakes. It was in my headlights for a few minutes, and we saw it clearly." While David was surprised, his friend was positively frantic at the sight of the bizarre creature. "It's a demon! They sent a demon after me!" he shrieked. When the monster darted into the brush by the roadside, David turned the car around to find an alternate route.

It took him hours to get his friend calmed down.

There were no other dire events, and in time whatever was going on with the coven either played itself out or was defused.

But David still remembers the thing that crossed the dirt road that night. "I saw it clearly in the headlights," he said. "I know this sounds crazy, but it was sort of a feathered serpent—about four and a half feet long, with reptilian scales, arms, legs, and claws, a serpent-like head and eyes, and feathers. It took its sweet time crossing

Why Did the Demon Cross the Road?

the road, sort of leaping along and stopping once to stare right at us. It looked like those carvings of Quetzalcoatl—you know, the mythic Aztec deity."

Good thing they drove away quickly; when Quetzalcoatl appears, he generally leaves with a human sacrifice.

SEE ALSO: The Awful

MAN-EATING STONE

LOCATION: Glastenbury Mountain

DATE: Prehistory to present

No one living has seen this dangerous anomaly on Glastenbury Mountain. Native Americans knew of it, and warned people away. We can only imagine it as a sizeable rock, large enough to stand on. But when someone stands upon it, the rock becomes less solid, and, like a living thing, swallows the unfortunate trespasser. A number of disappearances have been reported on Glastenbury Mountain. Could all these vanished folks have stepped inadvertently on that hungry stone?

SEE ALSO: Three-Hundred-Pound Bloodsucker

The MONSTER OF RATTLESNAKE HILL

LOCATION: Fair Haven
DATE: 1899

Hidden treasure on Rattlesnake Hill in Fair Haven was guarded by a strange wild animal. No one could identify it, few had seen it, but many people for miles around had heard its plaintive, piercing wail—it froze the blood, forcing people to keep their distance. But in 1899, three hunters—James Kelley, Fred Copeland, and Albert Austin—tracked the beast to its lair on "Bloody Ledge." They discovered the treasure it was guarding, thus setting it free. Or so they thought . . .

SEE ALSO: Buck Mountain Whatzit, Demon Boy from Hell's Half Acre, Densmore Hill Monster

DENSMORE HILL MONSTER

LOCATION: Hartland
DATE: Circa 1763 and after

Hartland has a tradition of monster sightings dating back to eighteenth century. The "hot spot" is Densmore Hill. It all started when Thomas Rood settled there in 1763. Some time later, the monster carted off the wife of Mr. Rood's son. Grief drove the young man to suicide. Mr. Rood never got around to describing the beast, so its appearance remains a mystery to everyone except those it has carted off or killed. All we know is that it's huge and has a peculiar manner of locomotion; it doesn't walk or fly, it slithers.

SEE ALSO: Buck Mountain Whatzit, Monster of Rattlesnake Hill, Quetzalcoatl

STEGGY

LOCATION: Bloomfield
DATE: 1970–1971

Although not much bigger than a large woodchuck, the creature spotted on a two-hundred-year-old farm in Bloomfield has baffled everyone who has heard about it. With jet black, shiny fur and a fat, long, pointed tail, it lumbered along, rocking side to side. Its rear legs were like those of a rabbit, but it walked heel-to-toe. Its haunches were tall and its front low, with "a longish body." Its small head jutted forward and was carried low on a line with its tail, which stuck straight out. Witness P. G. Lavigne* says, "Picture a very small stegosaur with no armor and black fur and you're close."

Mr. Lavigne had never seen anything like it. He says, "I spoke with an old hermit man at the end of the road who had lived there since 1912. He said that he had seen two or three in his life."

Bottom line: Neither man had any idea what he was seeing; neither has anyone else.

SEE ALSO: Green Swamp Monster,
Groton's Godzilla

WOODMAN

LOCATION: Jamaica
DATE: 1985 to present?

One summer day in 1985, Arlene Tarantino, then of Winhall, was relaxing with a book near Pike's Falls, deep within the Green Mountain National Forest. Suddenly, she heard a noise above the sound of the water. Looking up, she caught motion, as something substantial whipped past, violently disturbing the leaves in its path. Whatever it was jumped twice, landing about fifteen feet away. What she saw seemed human, but unlike anyone she'd ever seen before. He was naked. His body appeared thin and youthful, with conspicuous muscles, but his face looked old, craggy, and wrinkled. He had some body hair, but couldn't be described as "hairy." His stooped posture made estimating his height difficult; she guessed he was 5½ feet tall, weighing maybe 120 pounds. His legs, she says, were gnarled and ape-like, causing him to sometimes move "like a chimp . . . using all fours." All this registered very quickly before the creature took off. Arlene was impressed by his speed: He traveled "as fast as you could imagine," she said. "If you've ever seen a dog run so fast that it almost falls sideways, this is the speed that [he] attained." In a moment he was gone, leaving nothing but an odd story and the name Arlene created for her strange visitor: Woodman.

SEE ALSO: Bigfoot, Hopping Horror, Old Slipperyskin

SIDEHILL CRONCHERS

LOCATION: Bridgewater, Stockbridge, Mount Mansfield
DATE: Ongoing

These elusive monstrosities are said to reside exclusively within the deep, remote, almost forgotten Chateauguy wilderness near Bridgewater. Considered very dangerous, Cronchers are an unlikely hybrid: part deer, part wild boar. According to a description published by the *Rutland Herald* in 1966, "the Croncher has . . . short tusks, dark dirty brown hair, weighs at least 100 pounds, [and] has hoofs with prominent dew claws." They are well adapted to Vermont's hilly landscape, as their legs are shorter on one side than the other, depending on gender. This adaptation allows them to graze more comfortably on steep hillsides. However, because of this evolutionary peculiarity, they must always move in a clockwise or counterclockwise direction and would fall over if they turned around. One reason they are so rare is that breeding pairs must meet at the same elevation while circling in opposite directions.

Although they can travel at extremely high speeds, people can escape them easily by running straight up or straight down the slope. The Croncher will not be able to attack because it will have to circumnavigate the hill trying to catch up. Sidehill Cronchers (*Crevida scrofa*)—or something very like them—have also been reported in Stockbridge and on Mount Mansfield. Related creatures in other parts of the state are known as Sidehill Gougers, Rooters, Hoofpusses, and Wampahoofuses. These animals are so rare that no one has ever seen one.

Note

The Wampahoofus Trail above Butler Lodge near the Forehead of Mount Mansfield was so named by Professor Roy Buchanan because of a rock formation that looks like the profile of a Wampahoofus.

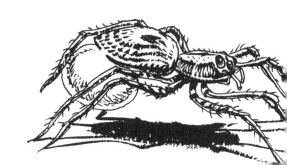

BLACK BEAST OF SNAKE MOUNTAIN

LOCATION: Addison
DATE: Late 1920s and 1930s

Probably this expanse of dense wilderness originally was called Rattle Snake Mountain because it was the habitat of Vermont's only venomous reptile, the timber rattler. Also, several varieties of unusual plants exist here, so one must ask what else may be lurking beneath the shaded cliffs or within the lightless vales of this 1,000-foot, 1,215-acre no-man's-land?

One report is of a black beast that supposedly roamed Snake Mountain in the 1920s and 1930s. This brazen creature often was spotted at night prowling around houses and barns. One specimen gave chase as a local woman, Isabelle Tatro, drove home after visiting a neighbor. She couldn't outrun the thing on the twisty mountain roads. Panicked, she pulled into the first farm she came to. When she stopped, the creature leaped on to her roof and began clawing at the vehicle.

Nearly hysterical, the poor woman laid on the horn. Ladies appeared on the porch and men ran from the barn to see what all the commotion was about. At the sight of the attacking monster, the women ran screaming back into the house, while the men raced to fetch guns. By the time they got back, the animal was gone. No one had any idea what they had seen.

Although not a witness himself, local stonemason David Cunningham heard a number of tales from his mother. One described how his oldest brother was chased by the thing. "He was about twelve or thirteen and had a job at a neighboring farm and rode his bicycle to and from work, coming home well after dark. One evening, as he passed under some tree limbs that hung over the road, something heavy dropped onto the road behind him with a thud and a grunt. Fear giving him extra strength, he peddled furiously for home, hearing a fleet-footed 'something' running close behind him."

When he got home, he raced into the house screaming for help. David concludes, "My father and grandfather went out with guns, but never saw any sign of the beast."

SEE ALSO: Buck Mountain Whatzit, Monster of Rattlesnake Hill

BENNINGTON MONSTER

LOCATION: Glastenbury Mountain and thereabouts
DATE: Ongoing

Descriptions of this incredible creature vary, but supposedly it is gigantic and occasionally can be provoked to anger. One fierce, stormy night in the nineteenth century, it attacked and toppled a stagecoach. After picking himself up, the driver looked around with his lantern. In the soggy ground, he discovered a line of tracks where something gigantic had passed by. They were widely spaced and deep. Whatever made them must have been of tremendous size.

The rattled passengers joined him to examine the prints, but no one could say what sort of animal had made them.

Just then, the four skittish horses reared and screamed.

Everyone saw two large glowing eyes watching from the nearby wood. A huge beast, partly obscured by tree branches and darkness, roared again and tramped off into the night, leaving the travelers silent and stricken with horror.

This creature, whatever it may be, has become known as the Bennington Monster. To this day, it occasionally pops up, terrifying hikers, hunters, and even motorists. Prehistoric or preternatural, the Bennington Monster makes its home in the Glastenbury Mountain wilderness.

SEE ALSO: Bigfoot, Goonyak, Old Slipperyskin, Windigo

Flash! Bennington Monster Finally Identified!!

In 1934, proof of the Bennington Monster was finally discovered—or so people thought. Workers at "Bar" Harbor's sandpit on Bald Mountain unearthed a number of large bones that folks assumed had come from a much larger skeleton.

News of the find spread rapidly through all the towns in the area. By the time the story got to Old Bennington, the bones were reported to have come from a "Brontosaurus Rex."

Sadly, when the fossils were examined by more knowledgeable eyes, they were identified as having come from a cow.

But a big one.

BUCK MOUNTAIN WHATZIT

LOCATION: Waltham (south of Vergennes)
DATE: Late 1950s, early 1960s

Called the "Buck Mountain What's It" or simply the "Whatzit," this unknown animal prowled the forests of Buck Mountain back in the late 1950s and early 1960s.

Buck Mountain (883 feet in elevation) is contained within a triangle formed by Maple Street to the west, Ethan Allen Highway (Route 7) to the east, and Otter Creek Highway (Route 17) to the south. It is a wild area, where things could easily hide and stay hidden. Locals who claimed to have seen the Whatzit—mostly hunters, hikers, and other outdoorspeople—describe it as resembling a goat with long, whitish-gray hair. But unlike any known goat, the thing runs around upright, on its hind legs. No one has reported seeing any horns nor could they get an accurate assessment of its size. When spotted, the Whatzit would run off screaming, easily leaping fences and other obstacles. Although there has been a lot of speculation, no one has ever figured out just what the Whatzit was.

SEE ALSO: Black Beast of Snake Mountain, Monster of Rattlesnake Hill

HUMAN-FACED CALF

LOCATION: Lunenburg

DATE: January 12, 1913

Evidence of this grotesque mystery from Lunenburg was discovered by Charles Jordan: a single postcard in an otherwise unremarkable souvenir album. Printed on the card, an inscription says, "The celebrated human calf, born in Lunenburg, Vermont, January 12, 1913." The picture shows exactly that: the body of a calf with a humanlike face. The fate of this "cow-boy" is unknown. After so many years, it's unlikely he would still be alive . . . if he ever was.

SEE ALSO: Batboy, Pigman

LONG-LEGGEDY CATS

LOCATION: Burlington
DATE: 1988

Mrs. Peduzzi's suspenseful interlude (see Black Panthers) is offset by occasional cat contacts that are more vexing than terrifying. Susan Lily* of Burlington had a weird experience that still puzzles her twenty years later. One summer night in 1988, she left her job at a local health club, then stopped at Wendy's Hamburgers on their way home.

As she pulled up to the drive-through, her headlights swept across the dumpster on the far side of the dark parking lot. The beams also revealed the legs of two animals heading toward the dumpster. At first she thought she was seeing some kind of dogs—pointers maybe—with very long legs and slender bodies. "But" she says, "they moved like cats and had feline lines."

Simultaneously, the two creatures leapt to the top of the dumpster—a distance of about five feet. No dog could spring upward in such a manner. As the animals peeked out at her, she became certain that they were cats. Susan says, "They were the size of a forty- or fifty-pound dog, but they were real slim and their legs were disproportionately long."

Susan has always lived around animals and can distinguish among different varieties of cats. These were something unknown. She says, "The largest domestic cat is the Norwegian Forest cat. But these were short-haired. They were much taller than Maine Coons. I have no idea what I saw."

As she continued through the drive-through, she looked back to see if they had come out of the dumpster. The creatures were gone. Although she made many more trips to Wendy's, she never saw them again—not there, not anywhere else.

SEE ALSO: Black Panthers, Monster Cats

BIGHEAD

LOCATION: Near Brattleboro
DATE: 1998

One evening in 1998, two women were driving north on the interstate near Brattleboro. From behind them, a convoy of three cars with bright headlights began to pass. When the middle car was parallel with theirs, its interior was illuminated by the last vehicle's headlights. Both women got a quick look at the peculiar passenger in its backseat: a grotesque, human-like being. It appeared tall, with a huge, bulbous, vein-covered head, pasty skin, and a spindly neck. What was it? Where was it going? Where was it coming from? The passing car with its odd occupant pulled ahead and vanished out of sight before the women could come up with any answers.

SEE ALSO: Monsters from Outer Space

BOWMAN'S GOLEM

LOCATION: Cuttingsville
DATE: 1891 to present

John P. Bowman's mansion in Cuttingsville is said to be haunted. The story goes that the aging millionaire exhausted his fortune trying to bring his dead family back from the grave. Then, after he had died, the remainder of Mr. Bowman's money was used to maintain a butler and maid who prepared and served a full dinner every night. Mr. Bowman wanted everything ready in case he, or some family member, shambled from the crypt across the street and arrived home hungry. Although his occult practices may have failed, one scary rumor remains: The statue of Mr. Bowman kneeling in front of his mausoleum occasionally creaks to life, lifting itself from the marble stairs and walking, in the subdued light of the moon, among the graves of Laurel Hill Cemetery. Apparently this ambulating statue patrols the grounds to make sure everyone is resting in peace.

SEE ALSO: Demon Boy, Man-Eating Stone, Monster of Rattlesnake Hill

INSECTOSAURUS

LOCATION: Alburg

DATE: Circa 1980

Don't step on this bug; it might step on you! An Alburg woman reports the strangest thing she has ever seen—a foot-long, bright orange, creepy-crawly that moves like an inflated inchworm. When flexing, the thing was a good eight inches high. It was covered with spikes and black spots. When observed, it was crossing the sidewalk. Where had it come from? Where was it going? What the heck was it?

SEE ALSO: "The Worms" Is Coming

STOMACH-DWELLING SNAKES

LOCATION: Montpelier and elsewhere
DATE: Nineteenth century

Because water purifications systems have improved greatly, the horror of stomach-dwelling snakes and lizards has decreased dramatically. But the possibility of ingesting some tiny living creature remains when drinking from springs, pumps, or rivers. In the mid-1800s, John Cooksod of Montpelier swallowed a salamander while drinking from a spring in a hayfield. It lived in his stomach for two years, greatly impairing his health. When his doctor gave him a powerful emetic, he vomited the living creature. It was 4½ inches long, bright red on top, with a flat head and shiny eyes. A newspaper cautions, "take care not to swallow these things, which go down so much easier than they come up."

THE DAMNED THING

LOCATION: North Pownal, Windsor

DATE: 1847–1955

In his short story "The Damned Thing," Ambrose Bierce tries to describe an invisible monster. He speculates that just as there are sounds the human ear cannot detect, so too are there colors we cannot see. "And," his story concludes, "the Damned Thing is of such a color!"

What "damned thing" was it, we wonder, that attacked the home of Thomas Paddock of North Pownal during October 1874? Suddenly his property was under supernatural assault. An invisible force rained stones down on his family, hired hands, and buildings. No one could detect the source of these projectiles.

And in Windsor, as recently as 1955, the home of Dr. Thomas Waterman was attacked by some variety of water-spreading entity. Puddles from nowhere began to appear. In the assault's first two days, the family mopped up thirteen buckets full. Many investigated, but no one could determine the source of the water. The situation got so bad that sometimes it actually rained inside the house. Eventually, the family fled this wicked water sprite.

In neither case was the attacker visible to the human eye.

frightening

VAMPIRES

LOCATION: Manchester, Woodstock, Burlington, Cavendish
DATE: Eighteenth century to present (?)

These life-stealing wraiths have long haunted Vermont towns, apparently beginning sometime in the eighteenth century. In Manchester, around 1790, Captain Isaac Burton's dead wife Rachel returned from the grave to feed upon his second wife, Hilda. Anti-vampire tactics such as exhumation and organ burning failed to rescue the doomed woman.

In October 1890, the most famous—or at least the most long-lived and universally publicized—case of Vermont vampirism was reported in the *Boston Transcript* and later as a page-one story in Woodstock's own newspaper, the *Vermont Standard.* "Vampirism in Woodstock," the headline said. The story told how, around 1830, a local man named Corwin died of consumption (tuberculosis). After his body was buried, his brother started wasting away. Common wisdom was that the first consumptive in a family to die was likely to come back as a vampire, his spirit rising from the cold earth each night to feed upon the essence of still-living relatives.

To determine whether the dead Mr. Corwin had returned as a vampire, town fathers ordered his body disinterred. Dr. Joseph Gallup, the Woodstock's leading physician and head of Vermont Medical College, observed that "the vampire's heart contained its victim's blood" (although exactly how he was able to determine that with any degree of forensic certainty remains a bit of a medical mystery).

There was only one way to stop the spread of evil: an exorcism. Dr. Gallup and his associates built a fire on the village green, heated up an iron pot, and cooked the corpse's undecayed heart, eventually reducing it to ashes. Then they buried the pot and ashes in a hole fifteen feet deep, and covered it with a seven-ton slab of granite. Before refilling it, they sprinkled everything with bull's blood, which they believed had purifying properties. Finally, they forced the dying Mr. Corwin to swallow a ghastly homeopathic medicine made of bull's blood mixed with some of his brother's ashes. Apparently it worked; as far as we know, there are no vampires living in Woodstock today.

SEE ALSO: Dummerston's Vampire Vine, Man-Eating Stone, Three-Hundred-Pound Bloodsucker

"THE WORMS" IS COMING!

LOCATION: Guildhall and beyond
DATE: 1770

Alfred Hitchcock's terrifying motion picture *The Birds* was a monster movie. Its uniqueness, of course, is that the monster was not a gargantuan beast like Godzilla, but rather a collection of tiny, lethal, normally docile feathered friends.

Vermont, too, had such a monster.

In the summer of 1770, invaders descended on the town of Guildhall. Inching steadfastly southward, innumerable in multitude, they were an army of worms! Millions of them, extending as far as the eye could see.

Everett Chamberlain Benton wrote in his *History of Guildhall*, they "extended from towns in this immediate locality to Northfield, Mass." Such an improbable flood seemed to signal the end of the world.

The hideous black and yellow striped worms were everywhere. Some were as big as a man's finger. They covered whole fields. As Rev. Grant Powers wrote, "a man could not put down his finger in a single spot without placing it on a worm."

The incredible crawlers carpeted the forests, blanketed cleared land, and polluted the wells. "[T]hey would go up the side of a house and over it in such a compact column that nothing of boards or shingles could be seen."

They entered and filled the houses. People found them in their larders, burrowed into bread dough, and twisted into the folds of their bedding. Clothing had to be shaken in the morning before it was put on.

In general, the worms seemed to be in a hurry to get—somewhere. They would pause only long enough to eat, and to the farmers of Guildhall, eating meant destruction. Worms leveled fields of wheat and corn, thus cutting off major food sources.

Then, around the first of September, the worms vanished.

Apparently the birds had come to the rescue!

Everett Benton wrote an "immense number of pigeons . . . came through . . . immediately upon the disappearance of the worms."

The pigeons fed on the worms and the famished settlers fed on the pigeons. It was a perfect balance of nature.

And it will remain that way.

Until it happens again . . .

SEE ALSO: Insectosaurus

BATBOY

LOCATION: Rutland and environs
DATE: May 1993

A colony of bats with near-human faces was discovered in a cave within the Green Mountain National Forest not far from Rutland. This is a most extraordinary discovery and it is hoped that The Nature Conservancy of Vermont will extend protection to the habitat of this rare and perhaps endangered species. For now—to protect the oddities—their location is being kept a secret. This remarkable find is attributed to Dr. Richard Clement, who successfully captured twelve of the creatures and moved three of them to his Rutland laboratory. Attempts to find Dr. Clement or his lab have been less successful.

SEE ALSO: Human-Faced Calf,
   Pigman

The DEMON BOY FROM HELL'S HALF ACRE

LOCATION: Bristol
DATE: 1800 to present

Around 1800, a pirate treasure (still undiscovered) was buried on Bristol Notch. As was the custom, one member of the bandit bunch was murdered so his ghost could stay behind to protect the loot. In this case, the victim was a boy who, over the decades, got angrier and angrier until he turned demonic. He and his sidekick, a fearsome hellhound, hold eternal vigil in the remote, sinister, and alluring region of Bristol called Hell's Half Acre.

Journalist Franklin S. Harvey provides the best description of this horror (circa 1860): "A boy with a frightful gash across his throat, [paces] round and round the glittering pile [of treasure] with a red-hot iron upraised to smite with a vengeful force the sacrilegious hand that dared to touch a single bar of the guarded pile."

SEE ALSO: Bowman's Golem, Fanny's Fiend, Green Swamp Monster, Vampires

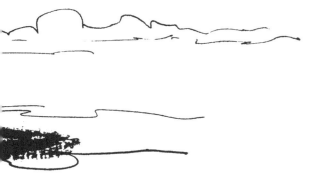

KING BULLFROG

LOCATION: Brandon
DATE: 1865

Well-diggers excavated a curious fossil from 114 feet straight down: a mummified amphibian snugly encased in a pocket of hardened mud contoured precisely to its form. Experts guessed that it had been preserved there for thousands of years. From nose to tail, this monstrous bullfrog measured fourteen inches!

Weirder still, the ancient animal began to twitch and jerk, spasming to life like Frankenstein's monster. Finally, it started hopping around. Eventually, some sympathetic townsperson seized it and brought it to a nearby pond, where it lived happily ever after. Its croaking could be heard for miles around.

SEE ALSO: Giant Red-Eyed Rabbits, His Snakeship, King Moose, Old Ironsides

DUMMERSTON'S VAMPIRE VINE

LOCATION: Dummerston
DATE: 1782 to present (?)

Around 1782 to 1798 in Dummerston, nine members of Lieutenant Leonard Spaulding's family were struck down, one by one. Upon burying the most recent dead—twenty-seven-year-old son Josiah—observers made an odd discovery: A peculiar gnarly vine or root was growing from coffin to coffin, connecting one corpse with the other. They concluded that each time the vine grew into the most recently buried coffin, a new person would die. Somehow, that villainous vine had united the dead to attack the living.

The vampiric blight was finally halted by severing the mysterious vine. Legend says it twitched, screamed, and bled.

But was that the end of things? Even today, some Dummerston residents fear a remnant of the vine might have survived. What if it takes root and resumes its evil work? Hopefully, enough corpses are buried in the graveyard to keep its appetite satisfied. But if it runs out of food, then what?

SEE ALSO: Vampires

WATER

VERMONT. . .

WILD WATERS!

CHAMP

Lake Champlain's
Watery Wonder

LOCATION: Lake Champlain
DATE: Prehistory to present

In the lightless depths of Lake Champlain lurks a creature unknown to, and unwelcomed by, conventional science—a monster. It apparently is alive. And big. Sometimes it makes its way to the surface, where it can be terrifying.

This, of course, is Champ, the reigning champion of all Vermont monsters.

Prior to the European intrusion, Native Americans knew that something weird lived in the water. They called it *Chaousarou*. Over the centuries, it has been seen by thousands of startled witnesses. Since 1609, when Samuel de Champlain sailed south from the Richelieu River, people have been keeping records of their sightings.

In the nineteenth century the creature was called "The Champlain Sea Serpent." That might have been an apt name, because many believe that it is a prehistoric holdover from the days when Lake Champlain was the Champlain Sea.

In the 1800s, newspapers were full of monster stories. In 1892, Captain Moses Blow of the Champlain Transportation Company had a sleep-shattering experience when he, his crew, and some passengers got a good look at "the serpent." It was a calm day, yet their boat rocked violently. No one could imagine what was causing it. All of a sudden, a head, neck, and back came out of the water. Whatever it was looked straight at them. Captain Blow said, "Let's get out of here," and they steamed off for Burlington.

That same year, "something" panicked a meeting of the American Canoe Association, sending terrified witnesses scrambling away from the water.

Such repeated confrontations inspired showman P. T. Barnum to offer a bounty of $50,000 for "The Great Champlain Serpent"—dead or alive. (That's about a million dollars in 2009 money.)

For a long time, people thought that they were dealing with a single dragon, a supernatural creature who had been a resident of the lake for ages.

But when considered from a more scientific perspective, it is clear that there would have to be several "Champs"—enough to sustain the population over centuries.

On July 30, 1984, the largest mass monster-sighting in history occurred near Appletree Point, just north of downtown Burlington. Aboard a sightseeing boat, *The Spirit of Ethan Allen*, more than eighty people, including the skipper, saw the critter.

In August 2005, two Vermont fishermen, Richard Affolter and Peter Bodette, made a video of an unrecognizable aquatic something. It moved in a "serpentine manner," leaving a series of corduroy-like ripples in its wake. At one point, it

The Soundest Evidence

A unique bit of Champ evidence came along at eight o'clock one chilly morning in June of 2003. A team of scientists from the North Carolina's Fauna Communications Research Institute, under contract to the Discovery Channel, were on Lake Champlain, shooting a documentary about Champ.

Lead scientist Elizabeth von Muggenthaler and Dr. Joseph Gregory were scanning the lake with highly sensitive underwater recording equipment. Suddenly . . . faintly . . . an unexpected sound came over the headphones. It was most definitely an animal sound, but it was something they had never heard before in Lake Champlain. If they had been at sea, the high-pitched tickings and chirpings would have been familiar—sounds made by dolphins or beluga whales.

But there are no whales or dolphins in Lake Champlain.

Liz and Joe moved to another spot and heard the sounds again. A third location revealed more of the same. The pitch of the sounds was incredible—ten times higher than any known fish in the lake.

What was it? We don't yet know. But one thing is certain: They had discovered a creature in Lake Champlain that produces unique and powerful bio-sonar.

"That animal must have the same type of advanced communication structures in the brain in order to create the echolocation, as whale and dolphin do," Elizabeth von Muggenthaler told me. "We can also tell that the animal can swim at least five miles per hour. That it does not appreciate sonar (it moved away immediately when we pinged). That it most likely uses the echolocation to find fish, and therefore likely is a carnivore."

Quite possibly they have recorded the sound of Champ.

surfaced beside their boat. The video shows something that looks like an alligator's head breaking the surface.

What was it? Maybe Champ, as the Champlain critter has come to be called.

Even today, Mr. Barnum's reward money is safe. Despite hundreds of sightings, photographs, digital images, videos, an audio recording, and the efforts of a growing gaggle of monster-hunters, the Champlain Monster is still unknown, uncaptured, and unidentified.

SEE ALSO: Connecticut Crawler, Fanny's Fiend, Mysterious Memphre, Seen in Bomoseen, Serpent of Dead Creek, Willoughby Wisp, Woodbury Water Witch

Note

You can't be too careful while swimming in Vermont waters. Monsters have been reported in at least the following lakes:

Lake Champlain	"Champ"
Crystal Lake	"Ms. Crystal"
Lake Elmore	"Elmo"
Lake Memphremagog	"Memphre"
Lake Seymour	"Seymour" or "Semoe"
Lake Willoughby	"Willy" or "Willoughby Wisp"
Woodbury Lake	"Water Witch"

Of course, we suspect that some of these may be imposters, trying to cash in on Champ's notoriety.

FUR-BEARING TROUT

LOCATION: Lake Memphremagog
DATE: 1957 and prior

This trout's fur represents a peculiar adaptation to frigid northern Vermont waters. The fur is invariably brown and the fish's size, large (suggesting that the pelt begins to develop at maturity). Because these fish are so rare, nothing is known of their primary food source, spawning patterns, or full size at maturity. Seen mostly in Lake Memphremagog, the last known specimen was caught by an ice fisherman in 1957. (Not to be confused with an Ice Fish, which is 99 percent water and likely to melt before you get it home.)

SEE ALSO: Fish Story

WOODBURY WATER WITCH

LOCATION: Woodbury Lake

DATE: Circa 1975

"(T)his reclusive amphibian, whose length has been estimated at anywhere up to 12 feet, generally lurks half-submerged in . . . quiet parts of . . . Woodbury Lake. While precise descriptions vary, a number of sightseers agree the Water Witch has a scaly body, a web-like tail and sports a forklike antenna . . . just above two large recessed eyes."

    Vermont Life Magazine, Winter 1975

LOCATION: Lake Willoughby
DATE: Nineteenth century to present

Infrequently reported, but never vanishing entirely, the Willoughby Wisp sometimes appears as two or three humps moving through the water. One specimen, killed by Stephen Edmonds in the nineteenth century, measured twenty-three feet long. In the 1950s, Navy divers photographed what they called "giant eels," six to eight feet long. On September 9, 1986, Audrey Besse and her mother got a good look at the Willoughby Wisp from a point in Westmore. Audrey reported a long, dark creature with two or three humps swimming south in the middle of the lake. By the time Ms. Besse readied her camera, the monster had vanished. Unknown animal? Oversized eel? Maybe both? Whatever lives in Lake Willoughby is most commonly known as "Willy." Unless, of course, people think it's female, in which case they call it "Willa."

SEE ALSO: Champ, Connecticut Crawler, Mysterious Memphre,
    Seen in Bomoseen, Woodbury Water Witch

So Where's the Proof?

In the early 1950s, the son of a wealthy Lake Willoughby family returned home on leave from the Navy. While he was sailing alone near Mount Pisgah, his boat capsized and the young sailor drowned. When his body didn't surface, the Navy sent a team of divers to find it. At around 300 feet, they discovered a lightless tunnel that descended even deeper. Inside, they saw—and photographed—giant eels six to eight feet long and as thick as a telephone pole.

According to the story, those pictures were kept by the Westmore town clerk. When I inquired, the assistant town clerk knew nothing about them. I then spoke with Mr. P. M. Daniels, who had held the post at the time of the drowning. He remembered the story, but not the photographs. "Could such eels exist?" I asked him. He said he thought it was very possible. In fact, he had seen one four or five feet long!

But today, the photographs, like the monster itself, seem to have disappeared.

A Note on Giant Eels

Vermont's giant eels are not confined to Lake Willoughby. They can be found in almost any body of water.

Lake Champlain holds a population of giant eels that are not to be confused with the Champ creature. Many people have seen them; a few have caught them, but nobody knows how big they can get. Dr. Philip Reines of the State University of New York in Plattsburg was scuba diving off Valcour Bay in about fifteen feet of water. He says, "I was just swimming along and I saw [something] in this area where people keep their boats. I said, 'What's that big, white, plastic pipe doing there?' I swam over to it and saw [it was] the biggest eel I ever saw. . . . It was about twelve feet long; it's dead white . . .'"

Giant eels can also slither up in more surprising places. For example, some years ago, divers were sent into the man-made canal at Bellows Falls to clean it of obstructions and potential pollutants. There they found what was essentially a writhing nest of eels. Giants? No one stuck around long enough to find out.

SEE ALSO: Seen in Bomoseen

MYSTERIOUS MEMPHRE

LOCATION: Lake Memphremagog
DATE: Prehistory to present

Memphre—the "water monster" of Lake Memphremagog—has an odd quality
not shared by its cryptid cousins, a quality that makes Memphre seem almost
. . . supernatural. That is, it has been described in remarkably different ways. Is
Memphre a so-called shape-shifter, an outsized amphibian glimpsed in different
life stages, or are there many different species of monster out there? A few typical
sightings—beginning around 1816—will illustrate:

In the mid-1800s, Uriah Jewett, Memphremagog's first monster hunter,
frequently saw a beast that became known as "Uriah's Alligator." Its name clearly
suggests the animal's appearance. In 1935, Dr. Curtis Classen confirmed this
diagnosis when he reported that an unfamiliar reptile crawled out of the lake

79

looking very much like an alligator. It was eighteen inches wide and about ten feet long.

In August of 1850, while fishing off Magoon Point, David Beebe was "astonished to behold the head and six feet of body of a huge monster. . . ." His conclusion: It was a giant snake. In the 1940s, witness Hector Guyon reckoned that the "snake" he saw was 150 feet long! For a while, this version of Memphre was referred to as "The Anaconda."

In 1972, Helen Hicks of Newport saw, "A creature that had . . . a face somewhat like a horse, with two very red eyes and a body . . . 75 to 100 feet long." And in July of 1976, a local fisherman saw what he described as "a seal with a long neck."

Are you beginning to see the pattern? No? Well, there isn't one, and that's what's especially vexing about Memphremagog's Mystery Monster. Unlike Champ, who is consistency described as a "water horse," Memphremagog's beast is seen in wildly different ways.

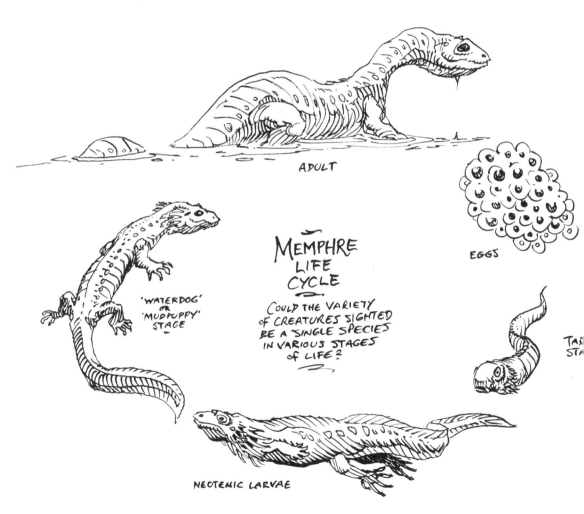

ADULT

EGGS

MEMPHRE
LIFE
CYCLE

COULD THE VARIETY
OF CREATURES SIGHTED
BE A SINGLE SPECIES
IN VARIOUS STAGES
OF LIFE?

'WATERDOG'
OR
'MUDPUPPY'
STAGE

TAD
STA

NEOTENIC LARVAE

Warning!

"Don't get too close to the water, or the sea serpent will gobble you up!"

Memphre is the only Vermont water monster ever described as dangerous. Supposedly it frightened the Native Americans in precolonial times, then went on to terrorize early settlers. Even today, old-timers remember their parents using monster tales to scare children away from the shore. Legend recalls an Indian who was devoured, canoe and all. In 1935, Newport mayor Frank Burns disappeared in the lake. Was he another victim of the monster's appetite? In the mid-1960s, some huge, snake-like critter surfaced near Hank Dewey's boat, then chased it all the way to shore! More dramatically, in 1972, Red Cross director Helen Hicks was relaxing with some friends on a boat. At around 10:00 p.m. she saw a horse-headed monster with glowing eyes. She said it was 75 to 100 feet long. The demonic intruder pursued the boat. For some reason, the motor shorted out and the creature submerged, leaving everyone terrified but unhurt.

This "Multiple Memphre" phenomenon was first noted over a century ago by an anonymous local poet:

Eyes saw the monster, but none saw alike,
He was half serpent, half horse, some said,
While others formed him like a huge long pike
With thick, bright scales and round, not flattened head.

(It's easy to see why the monster became more famous than the poet.)

Recent sightings of the critter only contribute to the confusion. Bottom line: Descriptions of the monster are so diverse that at least six distinct categories have been identified: the long-necked seal; the water-horse; the alligator; the "giant fish"; the "living log"; and finally, the snake or serpent.

So what are we to believe? Is Lake Memphremagog the most monster-crowded water in Vermont? Or is there just one Memphre, with a monstrous case of multiple personality disorder?

SEE ALSO: Champ, Connecticut Crawler, Fanny's Fiend, Seen in Bomoseen, Serpent of Dead Creek, Willoughby Wisp, Woodbury Water Witch

SEEN IN BOMOSEEN

LOCATION: Lake Bomoseen
DATE: Circa 1986

A man and his wife were fishing on Lake Bomoseen from their seventeen-foot boat. The motor was turned off and the lake was still. Suddenly, they both saw an extraordinary creature swim by. They described it as a giant eel, eight to nine inches in diameter, and easily two to three feet longer than their boat. That would make it about twenty feet long! They had no idea what it was, concluding it must be some kind of Loch Ness Monster transplanted into a quiet Vermont lake. Fearing that the creature might bite down on their bait, their boat, or themselves, they decided they'd had enough fishing for one day and got the hell out of there.

In consideration of this report, biologists Dr. Dwight G. Smith and Gary S. Mangiacopra said, "The size of eels varies greatly, but most mature specimens are reported at five to six feet with a weight of ten to fifteen pounds. Larger sizes are certainly possible, especially in landlocked lakes."

SEE ALSO: Connecticut Crawler, Fanny's Fiend, Mysterious Memphre, Serpent of Dead Creek, Willoughby Wisp, Woodbury Water Witch

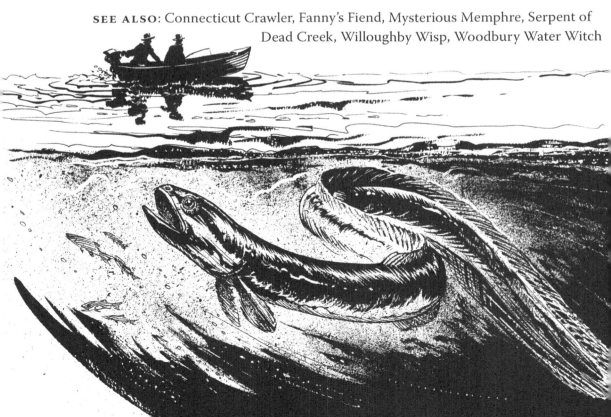

FISH STORY

LOCATION: Lake Willoughby
DATE: Ongoing

Besides the possibility of giant eels and prehistoric monsters, Lake Willoughby also is rumored to host an unknown species of gargantuan fish—fish big enough to gulp down a full-size man. The story is that they hang out in the deepest, darkest depths of the lake, lurking in underwater caves hundreds of feet below the surface. They never come to the top, so they cannot be responsible for Willoughby's infrequent monster sightings. In fact, the only people who have seen these mystery fish are divers who have tried to explore the underwater foundations of the sheer cliffs that flank the lake. So far, Willoughby's monster fish have eluded underwater photographers and seem immune to fish hooks, nets, and spear guns. So if you have an encounter with one of these leviathans, you want to be "the one that got away"!

SEE ALSO: Fur-Bearing Trout, Willoughby Wisp

THREE-HUNDRED-POUND BLOODSUCKER

LOCATION: Sharon
DATE: 1930s to present

In the middle of Vermont, within the vast Downer State Forest, there is an eight-hundred-acre woodland camp known as Camp Downer. And at its center there is a canoe pond constructed in the 1930s by the Civilian Conservation Corps. What lives in that pond is of concern to us here. It's something unnatural, something slimy, wet, and waterlogged, waiting for its next hapless victim. Campers and employees have long known to avoid a certain stretch of water behind the island. People vanish there, devoured by the monstrous mass that lies beneath the surface: A gigantic bloodsucker! A leech said to weigh at least three hundred pounds. We're not sure if that weight is estimated when the creature is hungry . . . or engorged. In any event, campers better beware. A run-in with this sinister slimer could be a real downer.

SEE ALSO: Man-Eating Stone, Vampires

85

FANNY'S FIEND

LOCATION: Westminster
DATE: Circa 1800

After the death of her father, Vermont hero Ethan Allen, Fanny, age twelve, moved with her mother to Westminster, where she enjoyed passing idle time on the shore of the Connecticut River. One day she had a startling experience. A terrifying monster came rushing through the water to devour her. Fanny said it was "of extraordinary size and horrid shape." Vermont historian Abby Hemenway

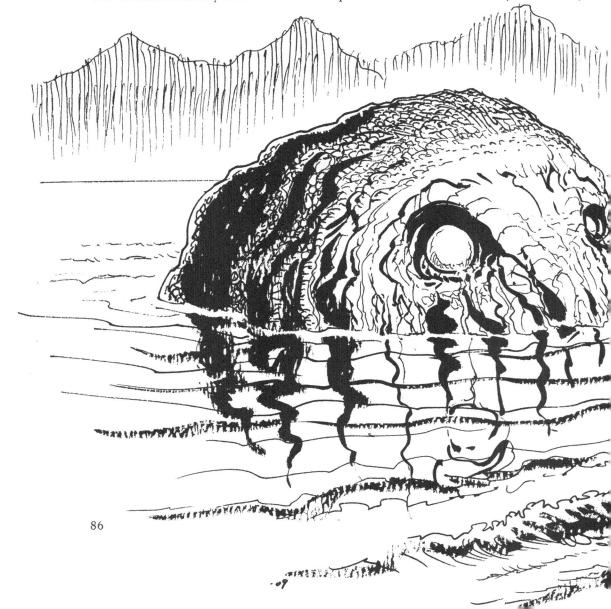

described it as a "monster of an aspect more fierce and terrible than the bear or wolf from the forest, and with widely distended jaws." For some reason—even as the thing headed up the bank toward her—Fanny could not move, only stare. Just before the horror could slash or bite her, an elderly man stepped out of the woods. He took her arm and said "My child, what are you doing here? Run away!" And she did. The monster about-faced and plunged back into the river. Later, Fanny became convinced that her rescuer was Saint Joseph, a belief that led her to the Catholic Church and to a life as a healer. The demonic entity was never identified. Apparently it could move about in the water and on land. Fanny's mother dismissed it as a bear. But if Fanny was right—that it required a saint to save her—Fanny's Fiend must have been a demon.

SEE ALSO: Connecticut Crawler, Demon Boy of Hell's Half Acre, Moore Lake Monster, Mysterious Memphre, Pseudosaurus (The Main Street Monster), Quetzalcoatl, Seen in Bomoseen, Serpent of Dead Creek, Willoughby Wisp, Woodbury Water Witch

SERPENT OF DEAD CREEK

LOCATION: Highgate vicinity

DATE: 1909

Perhaps the least well known of Vermont's aquatic anomalies is the one who resides in Dead Creek, which connects the Missisquoi River with Missisquoi Bay. Known as the "Serpent of Dead Creek," it was first reported in a 1909 issue of the *Swanton Courier* after it accosted three men out for bull pout. The beast was "big around as a sugar barrel." Supposedly it scared them out of their rowboat and up a tree. One of the fishermen said, "It was the tallest tree in the marsh, but it wasn't tall enough by a hundred, maybe two hundred feet."

He described the creature this way: "The top of the [monster's] head was black and hairy." It had "shiny gray scales about the size of a baseball on the throat, with big ones down towards the belly. When it opened its terrible mouth we could see several rows of glittering white teeth ten inches long . . . [I]t stuck its head out of the water . . . and sniffed a good deal like a bird dog."

One might suspect it was smelling something fishy . . .

SEE ALSO: Champ, Connecticut Crawler, Mysterious Memphre,
    Seen in Bomoseen, Willoughby Wisp, Woodbury Water Witch

CONNECTICUT CRAWLER

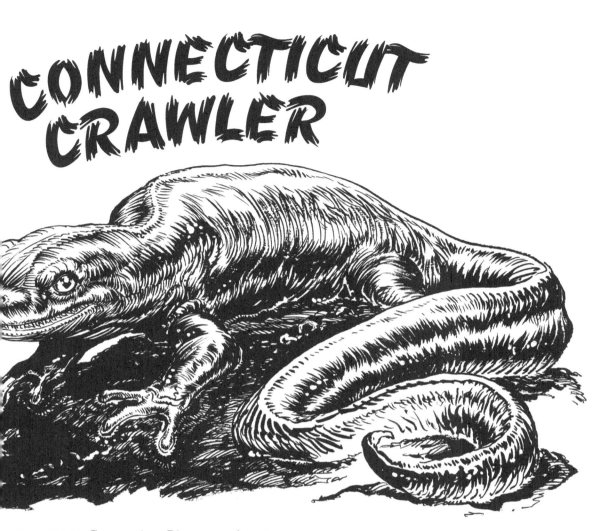

LOCATION: Connecticut River near Ascutney
DATE: 1968

In 1968, Douglas and Dorothy Gove were canoeing down the Connecticut River near Ascutney when they spied a small animal swimming beside them. It was between eighteen and twenty-four inches long with bright green scales. They agreed it probably weighed about two pounds. Eventually, they watched the creature vanish beneath a tree stump on the riverbank, leaving tracks and markings from its tail. The curious couple reported the incident to authorities at the state park in Ascutney, but no one could identify the tracks or recognize the reptilian creature that made them.

SEE ALSO: Champ, Fanny's Fiend, Mysterious Memphre, Seen in Bomoseen, Serpent of Dead Creek, Willoughby Wisp, Woodbury Water Witch

MOORE LAKE MONSTER

LOCATION: Moore Reservoir
DATE: 1968

Perhaps this is the strangest water monster of all. Whatever it is shows up from time to time in a wide section of the Connecticut River called Moore Reservoir, situated between Waterford, Vermont, and Littleton, New Hampshire.

The river was dammed to create the lake in 1957. The monster first appeared about a decade later.

On the night of May 19–20, 1968, three young people—a married couple and their friend—decided to go fishing. A little after midnight, they drove to an out-of-the-way picnic area and broke out their tackle.

It was moonless. Strangely quiet. The only sound was the occasional tiny splash of their bait hitting the water. When it became obvious that nothing was biting, their attention wandered. Suddenly, Michael Stinchfield pointed at a weird red glow on the water near some rocks that extended into the lake.

Moments later, Mrs. Hansen cried, "Look! Look at that!"

The red glow had left the rocks and was moving slowly through the water toward them. Now they could get an imperfect look at it. They later described a white mound, two feet wide, rising about a foot above the surface. Two glowing red spots in front looked like eyes. Something larger seemed to move behind the mound, but they couldn't make it out. What they saw they could only liken it to the head of an alligator submerged up to its eyes.

As the thing got closer, Mrs. Hansen and Mr. Stinchfield became frightened and moved away. Richard Hansen stood alone on the dock. On a whim, he cast his bait in the direction of the thing. Big mistake.

"It's coming at you," Mrs. Hansen screamed.

Everyone saw the thing racing through the water, coming at them. They scrambled for the car and sped away, slowing only to take one final look. Now the whole area around the wharf was glowing red.

The three immediately reported the incident to the Littleton police. Upon investigation, they found odd things. Most unsettling was a bunch of dead fish scattered around the wharf. Something had ripped them up, leaving only the heads, tails, and spines.

After that, monsters and red lights were big news for a while. Lately, things have been quiet. But there is a certain suspense in wondering who will be the next to confront the glowing creature in Moore Reservoir.

SEE ALSO: Champ, Connecticut Crawler, Mysterious Memphre,
    Seen in Bomoseen, Serpent of Dead Creek, Willoughby Wisp,
    Woodbury Water Witch

PSEUDOSAURUS

LOCATION: White River Junction
DATE: 1993 to present

You have a 100 percent chance of seeing this monster, or its bones, anyway. The specimen has a permanent place in White River Junction's Main Street Museum. Its provenance is a bit uncertain, although all indications suggest that the "vile creature [was] dredged from the waters of the

(The Main Street Monster)

Connecticut River" in 1993. Further, the Museum tells us, it has "baffled scientific experts at nearby Dartmouth College."

After the creature was first seen "frolicking" in the "lightly unsanitary waters just off of Lyman Point," the Museum dispatched an expeditionary party with the intention of capturing it.

According to a Museum publication, "A Herculean struggle ensued. In the end, all that needs be said is that the Remarkable Offspring of the Chambers of the Styx did not survive its attempted domestication. The matter was, however, put into the hands of our own Gulgo Vandershelz Bargain, a specialist in Oriental Taxidermy, who practiced his art with such magical skill that it can scarcely be detected that our Gargoyle Gave Its All for the Advancement of Knowledge. On close examination of the beast it was determined that Nature, up to her 'high-jinx' as usual, had beaten Human-Kind in marvelous inventions and created a Wonder."

(Therispod)

The Museum's documentation cites the following experts, who have tried to identify the specimen:

Dr. Li Shen, Ph.D., The Lab of Phenomenology: "This specimen, this remarkable finding, represents a here-to-fore un-delineated Evolutionary Link between the Gargantua of the Marine World and Modern Day Bovines."

Prof. Ria Blaas, Independent Researcher: "I have never encountered anything like it in all my long Experience as a Researcher in Micro-Terpsichoreans."

Zachary Blainford, M.D., Ph.D., Kresge Scientific Institute: "Since this creature obviously is not genetically capable of descent from any Known Earth Form, therefore it is my considered opinion that this Abomination must have been Teleported (by what means is unclear); as a type of, perhaps sinister, Extra-Terrestrial Biology Experiment."

SEE ALSO: Fur-Bearing Trout, Human-Faced Calf

GROTON'S GODZILLA

LOCATION: Groton
DATE: Late 1960s

The Desorta family, while visiting Big Deer State Park, encountered something that "looked just like a dinosaur." Jane Desorta described how it rose out of a bog, slowly crossed the road in front of their vehicle, and slithered down into a swampy, tree-crowded area on the other side. "Of course," she said, "the camera was in the trailer."

The creature was dark tan in color and close to the ground. It had a humped back, long tail, and arched neck. It was at least three feet high.

The legs were short and thick, with what Mrs. Desorta described as webbed feet—"Like duck's feet. Only they were *big*."

But when it comes to dinosaurs, what's really important is *size*. Just how big was this thing?

"From the end of its tail to its head was almost as long as the road was wide." That would make it fairly sizable; the road would have been eight to ten feet wide. An eight- to ten-foot lizard is a veritable Godzilla by Vermont standards!

Admittedly, it could be compared to an alligator or "a huge turtle that had lost its shell." But mostly—witnesses agree—it looked like some kind of dinosaur.

SEE ALSO: Green Swamp Monster, Steggy

96

GREEN SWAMP MONSTER

LOCATION: Saint George
DATE: 1784 to present

Ina Isham tells of the Green Swamp Monster that has menaced her family for generations. Their home was in Saint George, located between Mount Pritchard and Shelburne Pond, east of Route 116. Beside it, way too close for comfort, was a large boggy area known as Isham's Swamp.

Oddly, a fence surrounded the swampy ground. Why?

In the early 1940s, when she was old enough to be in the yard by herself, Ina's father warned her about the dangerous Swamp Monster that lived just out of sight among the trees. It was green like a frog, with unsightly black spots all over it, and long, brown hair. And it was gigantic! As big as two plow horses! If she wasn't careful, he warned sternly, the fearsome creature might dart out and carry her back into the swamp.

When Ina was six years old, the daily one-mile walk to school was a terrifying experience. Her father and older siblings told her to hurry along and to go quietly, so she wouldn't attract the monster's attention.

Sometimes, if curiosity brought her a little too close, she could see the monster moving under dry clumps of grass protruding from the fetid swamp water. Once she even thought it got into the house, but her father assured her it could not survive outside its own environment.

The threat of monster attacks seemed to diminish in winter. Her father explained that before the swamp froze over, the Green Swamp Monster traveled by way of a brook that flowed from their swamp to the larger swamps near Shelburne Pond. There it spent the winter with the other Swamp Monsters who came from all over the area.

In time, the true secret of the swamp monster was revealed. Ina's dad confessed that the Green Swamp Monster tale was a way to keep the kids safe from harm. He said it was better they be "scared to death, than be dead." Ina says, "He had been scared just like me, by his father Irving Isham, who in turn had been scared by his father, Gilbert Isham, who was scared by his father, Amasa Isham, who was scared by his father, Jehiel Isham, who [apparently] started the Swamp Monster story in 1784 when he moved to Saint George, Vermont, from Connecticut. It's possible the tale goes all the way back to England."

Well maybe so, but the original Vermonters, the Abenaki, had a similar tale. They told of an evil swamp monster who could be heard calling from the depths of the swamp, trying to lure children into the wet darkness where they would drown.

But in either case, the story is essentially true: Swamps are dangerous. And monsters are very, very old.

SEE ALSO: Groton's Godzilla, Mysterious Memphre, Three-Hundred-Pound Bloodsucker

AIR

VERMONT...

CAPTIVATING VIEWS!

LOCATION: Overhead
DATE: From then till now

A flying creature known to the Native Americans of Vermont, with variations reported all over the continent. Considered very powerful, Pmola is greatly feared, for it can swoop down and carry off animals or humans. It is generally described as big and bird-like, with glowing eyes and nasty claws. Yet, it can display seemingly human qualities. These winged wonders—or something very like them—occasionally are spotted today, but they have been around for a long time. The ancient submerged petroglyphs near Brattleboro depict giant winged creatures and also what appears to be a bird with seemingly human legs. Some form of this giant bird or birdman has found its way into the modern cryptozoologist's lexicon: we call it the "Thunderbird."

SEE ALSO: The Awful, Quetzalcoatl, Thunderbirds

PMOLA

THE AWFUL

LOCATION: Richford and northwest Vermont
DATE: Circa 1900 and ongoing

Known simply as the "Awful," this horrifying airborne unknown is spotted around northwestern Vermont, mostly in the vicinity of Richford. Supposedly it was first sighted one evening perched gargoyle-style atop the Boright building at the corner of Main and River streets.

Said to resemble a griffin, the monstrosity has gray, ten-foot wings. Its serpent-like tail adds another ten feet to its dimensions. Its nasty claws inspire instant terror. One of the first men to see it, a sawmill worker, was so petrified that he had a heart attack on the spot.

"You can usually hear the thing before you see it," a recent witness told the *County Courier* in 2006. " It makes a pretty weird sound, like a low scream . . . when it gets closer, you can hear its wings, which sound like fat blankets being shook out."

Other observers swore they witnessed it making off with a screaming infant. But no child was missing, so its unfortunate prey was more likely an animal.

More sightings followed. One woman spotted the Awful while she was hanging the wash. It scared her so much that she hid under her bed for hours.

Lisa Maskell, who grew up in the area, told the *County Courier*, "When I was about ten or eleven, we saw this thing sitting in a tree near the Trout River . . . it was huge with large wings and a long, strange beak." She thought it looked like a pterodactyl. "Big, scary, and fascinating."

As recently as 2006, a citizen of Richford spotted a winged monster swoop out of the sky to snatch a huge black crow. Was it a descendent of the original Awful? Or could it be the same critter still flying, now more than a hundred years old?

We may never know. As one witness said, "the general feeling is we don't bother it and it don't bother us . . . maybe with a few exceptions."

SEE ALSO: Quetzalcoatl, Thunderbirds

THUNDERBIRDS

LOCATION: Alburg, Shelburne, Groton, Irasburg   **DATE**: Ongoing

"That's no turkey vulture," the Alburg woman affirmed, watching in disbelief as the colossal bird soared overhead. It looked enormous! For years afterward, she'd say, "feelings of unreality, of strangeness, have persisted."

Like many other Vermonters, she had seen something that should not be in the sky. Something alive. Bigger than any known bird; almost the size of a small plane. Such encounters happen, but they are sudden and quickly over.

In the same area, another woman, Jenn Theodore* recalls something that happened in the 1980s, when she was eight or nine years old, "One evening in the fall . . . I saw a tremendous black bird. I remember playing near the swing set and looking up at a huge dark creature, flying very low. It looked to me like a prehistoric animal, and for many years I maintained that it was a pterodactyl."

Pterodactyl? Well, maybe the pterror part is right.

A Shelburne woman had a bit more time to study a monster in her backyard. This feathered phantom's head, sitting atop a long, thin neck, was a good three to four feet off the ground. Weird eyes stared at her while she stared back. Somehow the creature looked unpleasant, maybe even sinister. She had never seen anything like it. Too ugly to be an eagle, the only thing she could compare it to was the buzzards she'd seen in cowboy movies. But this thing was bigger, and decidedly stranger.

Finally, it just rose into the air and sailed off among the trees. This too puzzled her. Its wingspan was a good eight to twelve feet—greater than the distance between many of the tree trunks. Yet the bird flew without touching any of them.

Because of their seemingly supernatural qualities, some of these flying creatures have become associated with the devil. "Devil's Hill" in Groton State Forest got its name because, hundreds of years ago, a Peacham man passing by saw a gigantic dark bird circling above the hilltop. He swore it was the devil, so ever since that day the 2,038-foot peak has been known and Devil's Hill.

Stories of "Devil Birds" are numerous throughout the Northeast. They have been reported since colonial times. Even in the twentieth century, certain mothers in southern Vermont kept their children in line with tales of the "Devil Bird"—who might swoop down and carry them away. To many people, these stories were swear-on-a-Bible true.

In the early 1980s, Jim Guyette and his family experienced one of the most dramatic sightings on record. While at their family farm in Irasburg, they suddenly heard an unearthly screeching, unlike anything they'd ever heard before.

Jim ran outside and saw three huge birds flying toward them. Everyone gathered in the dooryard, gawking.

As the birds got closer, a sense of fear gripped Jim. These things were too big. Too unfamiliar. Their wingspan had to be at least fifteen feet! One headed toward a big maple tree in the front yard, where it tried to land. Perching was impossible, so it veered off. Its flapping wings shook the branches with the force of a hurricane.

Jim yelled, "Get back inside!" As he explained later, "I knew [those birds] were big enough to pick us up and carry us off!"

Witnesses included Jim, his wife Jeanette, their two sons, and a family friend. All watched the creatures fly off to the north, two in front, one behind.

What were they? No one knows. But all agree about their general appearance: sleek dark brown to black in color; heads disproportionately long and pointed, with elongated beaks and necks. Estimated wingspan, fifteen to twenty feet. Everyone said the wings seemed stiff, like bat wings. No one saw feet or legs, nor could they distinguish any feathers.

Needless to say, these winged monstrosities, sometimes known as Thunderbirds, appear nowhere in Audubon's bird book.

SEE ALSO: The Awful, Pmola

ORB of the VALLEY

LOCATION: East Fairfield–Bakersfield
DATE: Ongoing

In the East Fairfield–Bakersfield area, in the place known as "Lost Nation," there is a curious critter known as the "Orb of the Valley." It manifests as a seemingly intelligent ball of light. This basketball-sized, red, glowing sphere can move silently through the bushes, hover eight or more feet off the ground, or soar off into the sky. Occasionally, it will approach people as if curious, but it never allows anyone to get too near. It has been known to respond to human speech and, on at least one occasion, accepted an invitation to enter a cabin. What kind of creature could this be?

SEE ALSO: Monsters from Outer Space

MONSTERS from OUTER SPACE

LOCATION: All around us!
DATE: Whenever . . .

There is a long tradition of Monsters from Outer Space visiting Vermont. I guess the Green Mountain State is popular with tourists from everywhere. However, we will not devote a complete section to each variety of UFOnaut because they are by definition "alien"—we can be pretty sure they do not live here. And this is supposed to be a book about Vermont Monsters. But Vermonters do see these alien creatures, although in many cases they have no idea of what they are seeing.

Naughty Children

One case in western Vermont involved a farmer and his wife who suspected a bunch of kids were up to some mischief on their land. They crossed a cornfield to investigate, where—according to UFO investigator William Chapleau—they came across a landed spaceship. A woman stood in the doorway of the ship signaling for the couple to come on board. Instead, they ran home.

Buff Ledge

It was probably lucky that they did not climb aboard. In fact, my guess is that these invitations are rarely accepted, so the visitors had to start kidnapping people.

The most famous of Vermont's so-called "abduction" cases took place in Colchester, on Lake Champlain, at a girl's summer camp called Buff Ledge. It was August 7, 1968. A sixteen-year-old maintenance worker and a nineteen-year-old waterskiing instructor were relaxing on the dock and watching the sunset.

Glowing lights appeared over the lake, darting around like manic fireflies. One zigzagged toward them and splashed down into the water. When it emerged, it soared directly at them!

They could see small creatures within the craft's lighted dome. Later, the younger boy described them as having large heads, long necks, and huge eyes. The ship flashed some sort of beam at the teenagers, and the rest is a mystery. Or a horror story. Or a nightmare.

Later, under hypnosis, both recalled being taken aboard the craft and subjected to examinations involving scraping their skin and extracting fluids from their bodies.

The experience was terrifyingly real and shared by both teenagers. UFO investigator Walter Webb validated everything, as much as possible.

Not on TV

In Fairfield, at about eight o'clock one summer night, two witnesses were at home watching television. Through a window near the TV, they saw a bright light. They quickly realized that it wasn't a star, an oncoming car, or an airplane, so they turned out the lamps and television to get a better look. They saw a gigantic spaceship at least five stories high! They could see beings moving around behind its windows. The craft seemed to be hovering silently in the air, making it possible for the couple to see small, big-headed occupants that seemed to be conversing with one another. The story—and their memory—ends there.

Bedtime Intruder

On the night of January 6, 1990, a mysterious caped intruder visited a home in Townshend. At around midnight, the witness was awakened by someone standing at the side of his bed. When he groggily looked up, he saw a tall, spindly, almost-human-looking individual wearing a peculiar, high-collared cloak. The humanoid didn't explain a thing, but instructed the witness not to tell anyone about the visit.

Purple People Eaters?

Near Bennington on March 20, 1976, sometime around midnight, a couple in a car suddenly and simultaneously experienced an unfamiliar sensation. Inexplicably, their vehicle stopped. They watched two figures approach. The intruders were surrounded by an unearthly purple-colored glow. Almost instantly, with no sense of transition, the couple found themselves aboard some strange vehicle, where they encountered another being, this one encased in golden light. It communicated with them, closing its diatribe by saying that they would remember nothing of the event. However, they do remember the abduction happening, but recall nothing of what was communicated to them.

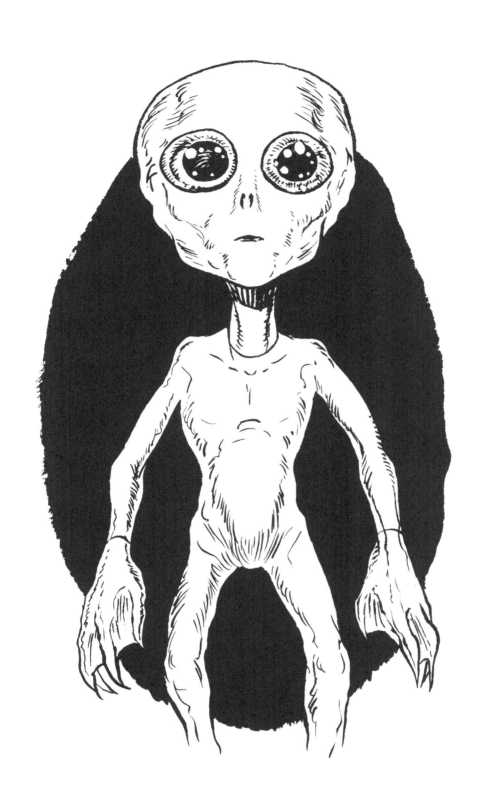

Seeing the Light

1999. Barre. 1:30 A.M. Police officer Alan George was on patrol. As he passed a wooded area, he saw something in the sky: an eerie glow that seemed to open and close in the darkness. He kept it in view as it gradually began to spread, eventually covering the whole sky. Now he could see vivid colors within the light—red, green, blue, orange. It became so bright that he had to shield his eyes. Officer George got out of his cruiser and watched, dumbfounded, as the impossible lightshow danced across the sky. Soon he began to see some kind of face materializing amid the lights: a longhaired man with a beard. An abnormally intense clap of thunder sounded and suddenly all returned to normal.

So what did the policeman see? A religious vision? An alien contact? A glimpse of another dimension? Or possibly a display of Northern Lights?

Space Boy

Robert Hurlburt recalls the afternoon in July of 1971 when he was hiking with his dog somewhere in the Green Mountains.

In a remote, somewhat desolate woods, he noticed a man sitting all by himself next to a stream. Surprised that anyone one else would be out there, Robert approached the man to be sure everything was all right. The young man seemed happy for Robert's company and together they walked uphill for a distance. Robert noticed his companion's unusual features: He was well over six feet tall, had odd-looking clothing, and spoke with an unrecognizable accent. Further, the young man—skinny as he was—didn't seem to get tired as they progressed up the steep hill.

After awhile, the tall man confided that he was just a visitor to Earth, that he had come from a distant planet with two moons. Its name was so odd that Robert couldn't remember it later. But he recalled that the planet was supposedly larger than ours, rich with vegetation, and comfortably warm all the time. The population was huge, although planned and carefully controlled. Healthcare was excellent; people lived to be 160 years old.

Needless to say, Robert couldn't believe anything he was hearing, so he asked for proof. The man produced a white object that appeared to be a polished stone, which he claimed was a communications disc used to contact his planet. It used body energy for power and transmitted like a radio.

When Robert touched the object, he felt a strong tingling sensation that ran from his hand to his head.

Not long afterward, the visitor mysteriously vanished.

No account of this story tells how the dog reacted.

SEE ALSO: Bighead

Monster Hunters

FROM JOE CITRO: Everyone knows the monsters are out there, but it took a team to find them. I would like to acknowledge the contributions made by each of the following people: Joan Alexander, Shoshana and Nicole Boar, Dustin Byerly, Allison and Brian Citro, Howard Coffin, Loren Coleman, John Coon, David A. Cunningham, Kevin Dann, Pete Fellows, Diane E. Foulds, Len Gerardi, Marie Goodrich, Michael Hahn, Jerry & Elaine Hinckley, Bill Hoyt, Ina Isham, Tom Kenyon of the West Windsor Historical Society, David Lepitre, John Mahoney, Gary Mangiacopra, Joyce Marcel, Scott Mardis, Gary Nowak, Aaron Pelton, David Pitkin, Shan Reil, Carole Renca, Ben Rose (Executive Director of the Green Mountain Club), Cath Monroe Sargent, Robert Schneck, Susan R. Shepherd, Cricket Smith of the Elmore Historical Society, Allison Templeton, Chris Wood-yard, Randy Williams (Fife Folklore Archives Curator Utah State University), and Lorraine Zigman. If I have left someone out, I hope you will accept my apology. Please attribute it not to bad manners, but to a failing memory.

FROM STEVE BISSETTE: I would like to acknowledge the life-long inspiration provided by the cartooning of Jeff Danziger, particularly Danziger's *The Champlain Monster* (1981). A huge thank you to my amigo and fellow cartoonist Cayetano "Cat" Garza Jr. for his fantastic work on the cover art, coloring my black and white portrait of Champ and following through our design concept to the final execution. Special thanks to Marjory Bissette; the Center for Cartoon Studies, Michelle Ollie, and the CCS Class of 2009, who provided critiques of some this work in progress; and most of all CCSers Mark Bilokur, Randall Drew and Jon-Mikel Gates, for overseeing, completing, and double-checking the scans of all the art in this volume. I would also like to thank the Vermont Institute of Natural Science, the Montshire Museum of Science, the Shelburne Museum and the Fairbanks Museum and Planetarium.

Finally, a tip of the pen to C. B. Colby's *Strangely Enough!* (1941), the late, great *World Weekly News*, Walter N. Webb's *Encounter at Buff Ledge: A UFO Case History* (1994)—specifically for the eye-witness alien sketches by UFO abductees Michael Lapp and Janet Cornell—and to the many artists whose work directly and indirectly fed and/or fueled some of the illustrations in this book, including Paul Bransom, Reynold Brown, Zdenak Burian, Harry Clarke ("Vampire Vine"), Richard Corben, Sam Glanzman , Jack Hamm, James Golden Irving, Joe Kubert, Martin Glen Loates, Roger Kastel, Charles R. Knight, Bob Kuhn, Samuel F. B. Morse (whose portrait

"Miss Jay" in the Shelburne Museum collection was the model for my female "Vampire" portrait), Rien Poortvliet, Cark Runguis, and Michael Zulli.

If I've inadvertently left anyone out, I stubbornly refuse to apologize, but will happily buy you a drink, here or in the afterlife.

TOGETHER, JOE AND STEVE would like to thank David Fairbanks Ford and the Main Street Museum in White River Junction, VT.

Last (and first too, if you think about it) the wonderfully creative UPNE team of Richard Pult, Eric Brooks, Amanda Dupuis, and Michael Burton.

You have all helped to keep Vermont's monsters alive!

Index by Location

Meet Your Monster Guides

Both native Vermonters, Stephen R. Bissette and Joseph A. Citro have worked together, as illustrator and writer, on the first edition of Mr. Citro's novel *Deus-X* and the *Vermont's Haunts Map,* as well as *The Vermont Ghost Guide.*

Artist Stephen R. Bissette, a pioneer graduate of the Joe Kubert School, was an instructor at the Center for Cartoon Studies from 2005–2020. Renowned for *Swamp Thing, Taboo* (launching *From Hell* and *Lost Girls*), '1963,' *S.R. Bissette's Tyrant®,* co-creating *John Constantine,* and creating the world's second '24-Hour Comic' (invented by Scott McCloud for Bissette). Comics creator (recently in *Spongebob Comics, Paleo, Awesome 'Possum*), illustrator (*Vermont Ghost Guide, Vermont Monster Guide*), author (*Teen Angels & New Mutants,* short fiction in *Hellboy: Odd Jobs, The New Dead, Mister October,* co-author of *Comic Book Rebels, Prince of Stories: The Many Worlds of Neil Gaiman, The Monster Book: Buffy the Vampire Slayer*), Bissette's latest includes *Cryptid Cinema*™, the '*Midnight Movie Monograph*' David Cronenberg's *The Brood,* sketchbooks *Thoughtful Creatures and Brooding Creatures,* and co-writing *Studio of Screams.*

ANYONE UP FOR SOME BAT SOUP?

Citro after midnight...

SKIN IS UNBLEMISHED BY THE SUN

Novelist and storyteller Joseph A. Citro is a well known collector of offbeat Vermontiana, concentrating on Cryptozoology and Forteana. *The Vermont Monster Guide* was chosen as one of the Top Ten Cryptozoology Books in the year of its publication, 2009.

For more than thirty years he has chronicled the oddities of local history on television, public radio, in his popular lectures, and in a series of bestselling books including *The Vermont Ghost Experience, Green Mountains, Dark Tales,* and *Weird New England.* He has also published five acclaimed novels rooted in legitimate Vermont history and folklore: *Shadow Child, Guardian Angels, The Gore, Lake Monsters,* and *Deus-X: The Reality Conspiracy.*

VERMONT...

Lake Memphremagog

North Country

Lake Champlain

Burlington

Mount Mansfield

Montpelier

Rutland

White River Junction

Bennington

Brattleboro

MONSTROUSLY FUN!

1 Alburg
2 Highgate
3 Richford
4 Lake Memphremagog
5 Morgan
6 Lake Seymour
7 Lemington
8 Fairfield
9 East Fairfield–Bakersfield
10 Irasburg
11 Crystal Lake
12 Lake Willoughby
13 Westmore
14 Bloomfield
15 Lake Champlain
16 Colchester
17 Mount Mansfield
18 Johnson
19 Morrisville
20 Lake Elmore
21 Wolcott
22 Craftsbury
23 Victory
24 Maidstone
25 Guildhall
26 Burlington
27 Shelburne
28 Saint George
29 Richmond
30 Woodbury Lake
31 Marshfield
32 Waterford
33 Lunenburg
34 Addison
35 Waltham
36 Bristol
37 Montpelier

38 Northfield
39 Barre
40 Groton Pond
41 Groton
42 Orwell
43 Lake Bomoseen
44 Brandon
45 Chittenden
46 Stockbridge
47 Bethel
48 Sharon
49 Fair Haven
50 Rutland
51 Plymouth
52 Bridgewater
53 Woodstock
54 Hartford
55 White River Junction
56 Hartland
57 Cuttingsvill-
58 Windsor
59 Cavendish
60 Mount Ascutney
61 Ascutney
62 East Dorset
63 Manchester
64 Jamaica
65 Bellows Fa'
66 Glastenbur
Mountain
67 Townshenc
68 Dummerst
69 Westminst
70 Bennington
71 North Pow
72 Pownal
73 Brattlebor

Made in the USA
Middletown, DE
14 July 2023

34883622R00073